MAKING WHIRLIGIGS & OTHER WIND TOYS

Sharon Pierce

Sterling Publishing Co., Inc.   New York

Cover design by Karen Nelson

Photography by Bonnie Benton, Ashland, Virginia

Library of Congress Cataloging in Publication Data
Pierce, Sharon.
  Making whirligigs and other wind toys.

  Includes index.
  1. Wooden toy making. I. Title. II. Title:
Whirligigs and other wind toys.
TT174.5.W6P55 1985   745.592   84-26782
ISBN 0-8069-7980-1 (pbk.)

Eighth Printing, 1986

Copyright © 1985 by Sharon Pierce
Published by Sterling Publishing Co., Inc.
Two Park Avenue, New York, N.Y. 10016
Distributed in Australia by Capricorn Book Co. Pty. Ltd.
Unit 5C1 Lincoln St., Lane Cove, N.S.W. 2066
Distributed in the United Kingdom by Blandford Press
Link House, West Street, Poole, Dorset BH15 ILL, England
Distributed in Canada by Oak Tree Press Ltd.
c/o Canadian Manda Group, P.O. Box 920, Station U
Toronto, Ontario, Canada M8Z 5P9
Manufactured in the United States of America
All rights reserved

To My Father with Love

A special thank you to

my husband Ryan and our children, Ryan, Randy, Christopher, Kristin and Kira, for all their love, patience and assistance.

Theresa, for her typing of this manuscript.

Charles Nurnberg, for his suggestion, without which this book would not have been written.

Maris Cakars, for his editorial assistance.

Karen Nelson, for her creativity in designing this book.

EDITOR'S NOTE

Patterns for some of the toys are too large to reproduce in this book. They have been reduced, therefore, by 25% and printed on top of a ¾-in. grid. To enlarge these patterns so you can use the sizes of materials given in the directions, buy 1-in. grid paper or make your own. Draw a portion of the original pattern one square at a time. Make the line running through the 1-in. square correspond directly to the line running through the book's ¾-in. square. After enlarging the pattern in this way, cut it out and continue instructions for making the poster-board pattern.

TABLE OF CONTENTS

INTRODUCTION

Welcome to the world of whirligigs and wind toys. The whirligig, an amusing relative of the weather vane, is a figure with paddle-type arms that whirl in the wind. Although these were used in the past to show wind direction and velocity, they were more often used as children's toys.

Although "whirligig" is actually a whimsical name given to certain wind toys, I have classified them in the project section as whirligigs if they have whirling arms or appendages. The rest of the wind-driven projects I have termed wind toys. Throughout the rest of the book the terms are often used interchangeably.

These fascinating, whimsical figures have entertained and intrigued both children and adults over the past few centuries. At present there are few whirligig makers, as can be evidenced by the scarcity of new original whirligigs. Primarily it is because little written material is available about whirligigs and wind toys, their history, and how to make them. In doing research for this book, I had a difficult time ob-

taining any information on whirligigs or any other type of wind toys. This book was written to fill that void and to inspire any would-be whirligig makers.

On the following pages you will discover how to make wind toys and what principles make them work. Complete patterns and detailed instructions are given for some unique and entirely original whirligigs and wind toys.

Truthfully, I have had a lot of fun designing and making each one of the whirligigs and wind toys in this book. Building moving toys is a very rewarding and fascinating pursuit. You will, as I have, feel a great sense of accomplishment each time one of your whirligigs first goes into motion. It is most enjoyable to observe the raw piece of wood that you first start with and then have it take shape into one of the following projects. None of the projects are difficult or very time-consuming. However, a little patience is needed when working on the balance and freedom of movement.

I strongly encourage you to try designing your own whirligigs and wind toys. And if you are interested in producing a carved whirligig, the patterns are basic enough for roughing-out a figure.

The projects in this book can be used as decorative folk art pieces or as working wind toys.

"Thus while the busy dame bustled about the house, or plied her spinning wheel at one end of the piazza, honest Balt would sit smoking his evening pipe at the other, watching the achievements of a little wooden warrior, who, armed with a sword in each hand, was most valiantly fighting the wind on the pinnacle of the barn." *The Legend of Sleepy Hollow,* Washington Irving (1819)

HISTORY OF WIND TOYS

Wind. From the beginning of time, it has intrigued man with its ability to change in a moment's notice. Like a child with a temper tantrum, the wind can alter itself from a cooling, soothing breeze into a terrifying, devastating force able to ravage the land and the people on it.

As early as the twentieth century B.C. the Babylonians learned to use this great power. Emperor Hammurabi used a windmill for irrigation purposes and eventually man used the windmill to grind his wheat. Records confirm that windmills were operating in many of the European countries by the year 1000 A.D. It was the Europeans who took greatest advantage of the windmill and improved its design and usefulness.

Watching these wind-powered paddles was probably the inspiration that prompted the first whirligig to be made. It is not known exactly when or by whom the first was made; however, a small number of whirligigs were known to exist in Germany, Holland, France, and England in the 18th century. It is in America, though, that the whirligig grew most in popularity.

Although whimsical in nature, whirligigs and other wind toys had a practical use as well. Just as the weather vanes were used to tell direction of the wind, whirligigs were used at times as indicators of wind velocity. The stronger the wind, the faster they whirled. Whirligigs have also been referred to as "Sunday toys." Considering that in the past play on Sundays was restricted to "quiet" toys, these would have been a good choice.

Because many whirligigs and wind toys are carved, they fall into the category of folk art. Many serious folk art collectors have at least one whirligig in their collection. Since all wind toys are rather fragile by their nature, with thin wooden paddles or propellers, very few from the past have remained intact. Most that have can only be found in museums or private collections.

DIRECTIONS FOR USE

There are a few essential points to remember in order to make a whirligig or wind toy that works properly. The first item necessary, of course, is the wind. Wind toys, like weather vanes, should be mounted in a place free of obstructions. If your house is situated close to other buildings, it is best to place your wind-propelled toy up high. This is why weather vanes and whirligigs were most often found on rooftops. Be sure to observe the wind patterns around the position you plan to place your wind toy before permanently stationing it there.

The second, and most important aspect, is that the wind must hit the propeller or paddle at the angle or side that it was designed to or it will not work. A good example of this is the windmill which is turned into the wind by the use of a tail vane so that the wind blows directly into the paddles. The solid paddle whirligigs can be operated by catching the wind from four different directions. Also note that the flat side of the whirligig, like a weather vane, will cause the wind to blow the whirligig into it.

A third consideration, also of utmost importance, is correct balance. The paddles must be almost identical in weight and shape for even distribution of the weight. If they are not balanced well the axle rod will not move freely. Ideally one paddle should be slightly heavier so that one is up and the other down. The wind catches it easier in this position. Each set of paddles is a little different, so it is best to test them on a "dummy" whirligig for movement.

The axle of the whirligigs and the propellers of the other wind toys must operate with as little friction as possible. There must also be free movement of the whirligig or wind toy at the point where it rests on the pivot rod. For this reason the whirligig people should have a small base, approximately 1¼ in. by 3 in. which is cut from ⅜-in. or ½-in. wood. A piece of wood this small can be split from a ¾-in. thickness with the band saw. A hole should be drilled in the base to correspond with the hole on the underside of the whirligig. The pivot post is placed through the base first and then into the

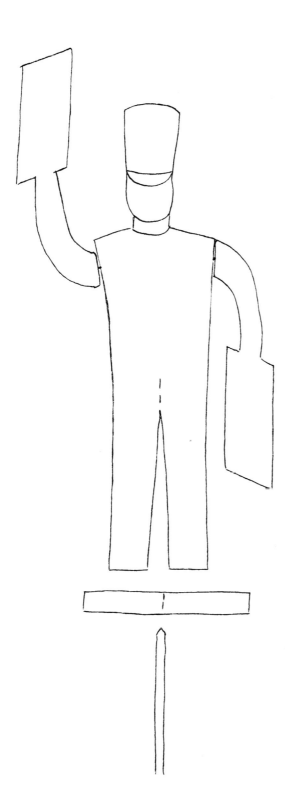

toy. The base is glued to the bottom of the whirligig (Illus. 1). This keeps the figure from wobbling.

Illus. 1. Base for whirligig people when used outdoors

GENERAL INSTRUCTIONS

The steps you will be taking in order to complete a whirligig or other wind toy are: making a pattern; cutting softwood with a band saw or scroll saw; sanding with the use of a sanding device and also by hand; drilling; painting. The most critical of these steps are the sanding and the drilling, as these are the two steps that contribute to the balance of the paddles.

The whirling mechanism is the most important part of your project. When making a whirligig you will be using one of three distinctly different whirling mechanisms: the solid paddle, the attached paddle, or the propeller. A pair of one of these types will be needed for each whirligig.

The shoulder, arm, and paddle are a continuation of one another and are cut from one piece of wood in the solid paddle. There are two variations of this type. The first has two identical angled paddles, which when positioned on opposite sides of the whirligig will be a mirror image of the other. These are attached with one paddle up and one paddle down (Illus. 2). The other has two flat paddles, one facing front, the other facing the side. These are also positioned one up and one down when attached to the shoulder axle (Illus. 3).

The attached paddle consists of an arm which extends straight out from the shoulder axle and a paddle. The arm is either notched or drilled on the end to hold the paddle which is placed at an angle. On one side the paddle extends up, while on the other side it points down (Illus. 4).

The whirligig propeller can be made in two different ways. The first starts with a solid length of wood. Approximately one-third of the wood on either end is sanded to an angle. While one side is angled to the left, the other side is angled to the right (Illus. 5).

The second technique uses three separate pieces of wood. Two wing shapes are cut from thin wood, approximately ¼ in.

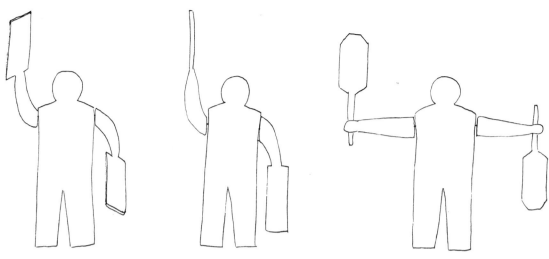

Illus. 2. Solid paddle, angled   *Illus. 3. Solid paddle, sanded front, side*   *Illus. 4. Attached paddle*

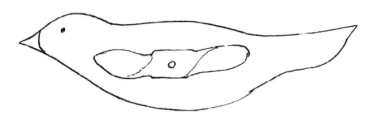

Illus. 5. Solid propeller

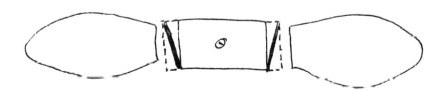

Illus. 6. Pieced propeller

thick. Then a small block of wood is grooved on both ends at an angle, from corner to corner (reverse angles), to hold the wings (Illus. 6). When the wings are attached, if they are identical on both sides of the whirligig, the wings will move in the same direction. However, if they are fastened as a mirror image, they will whirl in opposite directions. The propellers are attached independent of each other.

For the wind toys, you will be using three different whirling devices. The first of these is a four-blade propeller which is fashioned out of two lengths of wood and sanded so that each piece has two reverse paddles. These are joined after a section is cut from the middle of each. When rotating, the blades will have the same angle (Illus. 7).

The second type of wind toy uses a wheel cut from copper or aluminum. Eight cuts are made towards the center and then each section is flared in the same direction. This method was used for the bicycle and the umbrella (Illus. 8).

Only one of the wind toys in this book makes use of the last technique and that is the paddle wheel. Notches are cut out of a wooden circle and thin rectangular paddles are inserted. As with all the wind toys, this must be very well balanced and free-moving (Illus. 9).

The majority of the whirligigs in this book have the solid paddle. It is very useful if you construct a "dummy" whirligig out of scrap wood and then use this to

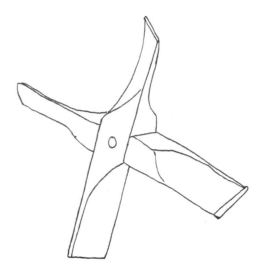

Illus. 7. Four blade propeller

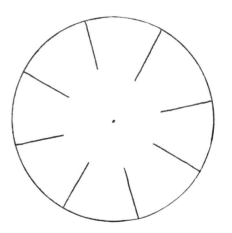

Illus. 8. Flared wheel

check the balance and movement of your paddles (Illus. 10). A small fan is handy for this testing as the wind is not always obliging. However, if it is a windy day, test outdoors.

When making one of the solid paddle whirligigs, here are three steps to be given extra attention:

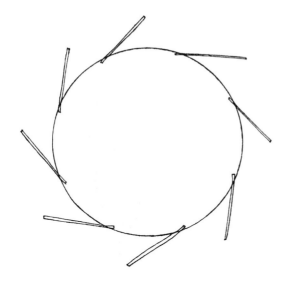

Illus. 9. Paddle wheel

Illus. 10. Dummy whirligig

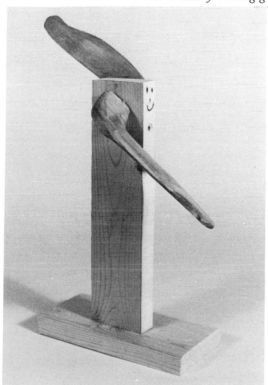

Shaping the Paddle

As mentioned in each set of instructions, you must mark a pencil line at the bottom of the paddle from corner to corner. This will give you a guide to use when sanding. The paddles may be flattened to this angle by using only the sander, but it is quicker to use the band saw if you are making one of the paddles that is not much wider than the thickness of the wood. Set the table of the saw at a 45° angle to the blade and make a cut on either side of the pencil line, leaving at least a 3/16 in. thickness for the paddle (Illus. 11). Straighten the table of the saw and then remove the section on each side of the paddle that has not fallen away yet by cutting in to meet the original cuts (Illus. 12). Whichever method is used to make the paddles, make two identical paddles and sand them to between 1/8 in. and 3/16 in. (do not flatten the shoulder).

Shoulder Axle

The hole that is drilled for the rod through the shoulder section must be drilled as straight and as centered as possible. If the rod you use varies from the dimensions recommended, be sure when you drill the hole that it is only slightly larger than the rod you use. Optional: insert a plastic tube or a drinking straw that is just large enough to house the rod, but still allows free movement.

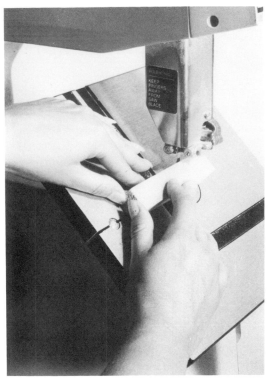

Pivot Rod

This rod is necessary for every one of the whirligigs and wind toys in order to move into the wind freely. The metal rod suggested here is ³⁄₁₆ in. in diameter. Once again, the hole that is drilled must be perfectly straight so that the whirligig can move properly. This hole should also be only slightly larger than the rod. For ease of movement, file the end of the rod to a dull point. Cut off the top ⅜ in. of a flathead tack or nail and insert it into the hole so that the rod will rest on the flat surface (Illus. 13).

Illus. 11. Cutting solid paddles with band saw

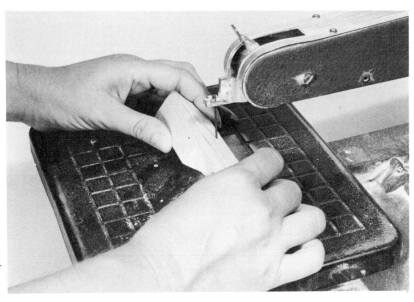

Illus. 12. Cutting off excess from first cut

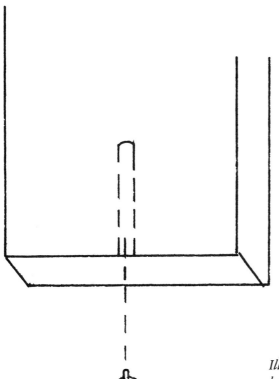

For your first project, I would suggest one of the whirligigs with a propeller type paddle, such as the grasshopper, Canadian goose, or raven. These are the easiest, and of the three, the raven would be the simplest to paint and it would also let you try paddle sanding.

Illus. 13. Inserting top of flat-head tack

FINISHES

All the projects in this book have been painted with acrylic tube paints. These paints are easy to work with, dry quickly, and are permanent once dry.

If you will be using your whirligigs and wind toys primarily as folk art, there are three basic ways to finish them. The first choice is to paint the item with the acrylic paint suggested and merely let it

Illus. 14.
Three finishes

dry. With this method, you allow the paint to age naturally with time. This is the only step, but it is also the first step in the other two techniques.

The next option is to rub a medium-color stain over the piece after the paint has dried. This will give it an aged look.

The third way to finish the whirligig or wind toy and create a very old, worn appearance is to sand the entire whirligig with fine sandpaper after the paint has dried. Make sure to remove a little paint around the edges. This will enhance the carved look. Then apply a light coat of medium-color stain, rubbing off the excess (Illus. 14).

The differences are quite impressive. Whichever type finish you choose, be sure to complete the finish with a protective coat of semi-gloss lacquer spray or other sealer. If the wind toy will be used outdoors, rub with steel wool and apply a second coat of sealer. Another choice for outdoor use is enamel paints as these are very durable.

MATERIALS & EQUIPMENT

This is a summary of the materials and equipment you will need to make the various whirligigs and wind toys. Some of the projects do not require all of the materials listed; however, a description of the essential details is given.

Materials

WOOD

For the majority of the projects ¾-in. white pine is used. Occasionally ⅜-in. pine is used. Select a board that is straight and free of splits. Lay patterns lengthwise, with the grain.

WOODEN DOWELS

Several of the projects require ³⁄₁₆-in. or ⅝-in. dowels. Occasionally, a ⅛-in. dowel is used.

METAL RODS

Use ⅛-in. diameter rods for the shoulder axles and ³⁄₁₆-in. diameter for the pivot rods. These can usually be purchased at a hobby shop or hardware dealer's. The rods I used are brass.

COPPER/ALUMINUM

A small piece of sheet metal, either .015 × 10 in. or .025 × 10 in. These are needed for the bicycle wheel.

SANDPAPER

Use medium-grade paper for the majority of sanding, including paper for the sander. Final sanding should always be done by hand, with a fine-grade sandpaper.

PAINT

All projects made for decorative use are painted with acrylic tube paints. These paints are permanent once dry and could be used for outdoors. However, enamel paint would be more durable outside.

STAIN

For a few of the whirligigs stain is used for paddles and skin color. It is also used if you desire an aged appearance. Choose a medium-color stain and apply only a light coat. Immediately wipe off the excess.

SEMI-GLOSS LACQUER SPRAY
Use this as a protective coating on all projects.

BRUSHES
Brushes needed are ¾ in., ½ in., ¼ in. and a very small round ¹⁄₁₆ in. Use only quality brushes. They wear well and are easier to paint with.

WOOD GLUE
Yellow wood glue should be used, particularly if the wind toys will be used outdoors. This is only required on a couple of the projects.

EPOXY GLUE
Glue the shoulder axle to the shoulder of the solid paddles with this. Insert into holes using a toothpick.

EMERY CLOTH
This is abrasive cloth for sanding metal edges. Use it to sand the pivot rods to a dull point. It is also used for sheet metal edges.

FLATHEAD WOOD SCREWS
These are used in sizes 1½ in. × 6, 2 in. × 6 and 2½ in. × 6 for the whirligigs and wind toys with propellers.

FLATHEAD NAILS OR TACKS
Flathead is used as a spinning surface for the pivot rods.

WASHERS
Various sizes with small openings are used to increase mobility and reduce friction.

BRASS ESCUTCHEON PINS
Small ⅝-in. brass tacks, with rounded head.

COPPER WIRE
Use 14 gauge for the Boy on Bicycle.

THIN BRASS ROD
A ¹⁄₃₂-in. diameter rod, flexible enough for the Grasshopper antennae.

TRACING PAPER
This is used to trace the patterns from this book.

POSTER BOARD (thin cardboard also known as "oak tag")
Make pattern templates with this.

Equipment

GOGGLES
Always wear eye protection when cutting, sanding, or drilling.

DUST MASK (optional)
Recommended for woodworking, as dust particles can be a health hazard.

TABLETOP SCROLL SAW OR BAND SAW
The scroll saw has a vibrating blade and is especially useful for small intricate work. Choose a finetooth blade. My scroll saw has a shaft for a sanding wheel, which I use for most of my sanding.

A band saw has a thin continuous blade. A small, hobby band saw is sufficient for the cutting involved in this book. Choose a ⅛-in. blade for intricate work, ¼ in. for straight cuts. A metal cutting blade is required for two of the projects.

SANDER

Choose either a sanding disc, as on the scroll saw, or a small stationary belt sander. Use medium-grade sandpaper. Sand all edges, except paddles, as round as possible, striving for a carved appearance.

DRILL

Any portable hand drill is suitable. Drill bits needed are $\frac{1}{8}$ in., $\frac{1}{16}$ in., $\frac{3}{16}$ in., $\frac{3}{32}$, $\frac{5}{32}$, $\frac{7}{32}$ and $\frac{9}{64}$ in.

EXTENDED DRILL BIT

Either $\frac{7}{32}$ in. or $\frac{3}{16}$ in.

METAL CUTTERS

These are needed to cut the metal rods.

DRILL PRESS

This is a great aid for drilling straight and accurate holes.

KEYHOLE SAW

A small hand-held saw used in lieu of a scroll saw for two of the projects requiring internal cuts.

HOT GLUE GUN

This piece of equipment is used for temporarily attaching the paddles while testing movement. They are available at most hardware dealers and crafts shops.

Whirligigs: Solid Paddle

Illus. 15.

Soldier

MATERIALS

Pine, ¾ in. thick: 9 × 12½ in.

Pine, ⅜ in. thick: 1 × 2¼ in.

Wood 2 × 4 : 4⅛ in. long (optional base piece)

Metal rod, ⅛ in. diameter: 3½ in. long

Metal rod, 3/16 in. diameter: 6½ in. if to be mounted on base or 15 to 36 in. if not

Brass escutcheon pins, ½ in. × 18: eight

Acrylic paint: titanium white, burnt umber, naphthol red light, mars black, raw umber

Sandpaper: medium and fine grades

Emery cloth

Brushes: ½ in. and ¼ in.

Epoxy glue

Wood glue

Tracing paper

Poster board

Semi-gloss lacquer spray

TOOLS

Scroll saw or band saw

Drill with ⅛, 9/64, 3/16, and 7/32-in. bits

Extra length 7/32-in. drill bit (if not available, use an extra length 3/16-in. bit)

Stationary belt sander or sanding wheel: with medium-grade sandpaper

Metal cutters

Hot glue gun (optional): for testing paddles on dummy

INSTRUCTIONS

Pattern. Trace pattern pieces and transfer onto poster board, including all paint lines. Cut out templates, cutting outline only. Trace the pattern of the soldier and the two paddles onto ¾-in. pine.

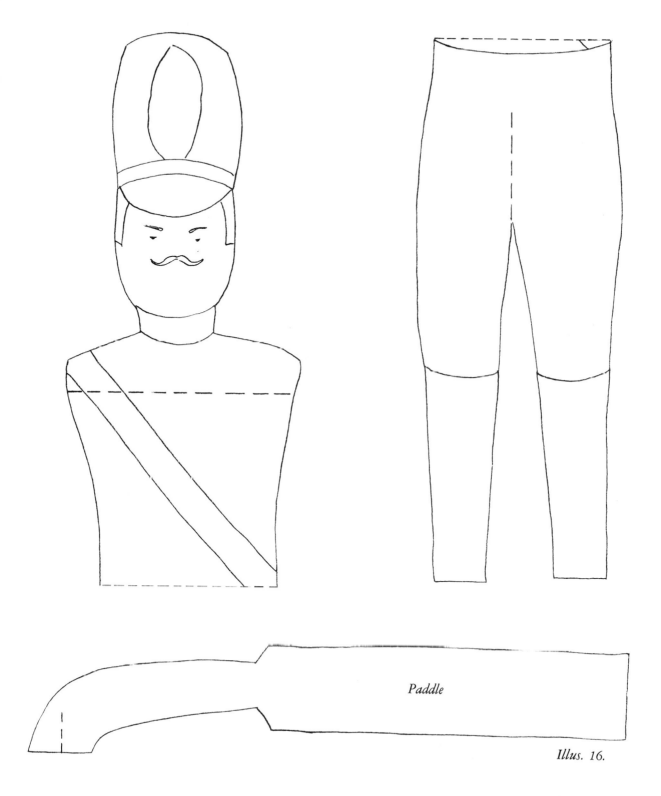

Paddle

Illus. 16.

Cutting. Out of the ¾-in. wood, cut the soldier pieces and also a 3 × 3-in. square for the base. Cut out a 1 × 2¼-in. piece from ⅜-in. wood and a 4⅛-in. length of 2 × 4.

Drilling. Drill a ⅛-in.-diameter hole into the shoulder part of the paddles as marked. All holes must be drilled with precision, as straight and as centered as possible. I suggest the use of a drill press, if you have access to one. Using the ⁹⁄₆₄-in. drill bit, drill a hole for the axle, through the body of the soldier, as marked. These holes are critical for balancing the paddles. Using the ⁷⁄₃₂-in. extra length drill bit, drill as indicated between the legs. This is for the pivot rod. With the regular length ⁷⁄₃₂-in. bit drill a hole through the center of the ⅜-in. base. Drill a ³⁄₁₆-in. hole into the center of the 3 × 3-in. base piece. This will enable the soldier to move freely while the rod remains stationary in the base. Cut off the top ⅜-in. flathead of a tack with metal cutters and insert this, flat side out, into the hole that will house the pivot rod. Tap it in with a dowel (Illus. 13, p. 17).

Shaping Paddles. To form the soldier's paddles first draw an angle line with a pencil from the top right corner to the bottom left corner on the end of each paddle. Hold the paddles side by side and make sure the paddles and angle lines are identical. It needs to appear that you are making two right arms/paddles; however, when placed on the other side the arm will be reversed as it should be. You may take a shortcut by using the band saw to remove some of the excess wood from the paddle (See p. 12, General Instructions) and then proceed with the sanding as described here, or you may do the entire shaping with the sander.

Always paying attention to the drawn pencil angle, take the paddle in your hand and gently press it against the sander. Keep the pencil line *parallel* to the sander at all times. Move the paddle back and forth against the sander. After you have sanded a portion away on one side, turn the paddle over and start sanding on the other side. Keep sanding both sides until you reduce the paddle (not the shoulder) to approximately ⅛ to ³⁄₁₆ in. It is very important to keep checking the angle (Illus. 42). I prefer the sanding wheel, as I can see the angle more easily. Repeat this procedure with the other paddle, making them as identical as possible.

Sanding. Round the shoulder and arm of the paddles as much as possible with the sander. Also round the body edges, holding the edges at an angle to the sander to achieve a carved appearance. Sand all base pieces. Give each piece a final sanding by hand with fine sandpaper.

Testing. Make a "dummy" whirligig out of ¾-in.-thick scraps of wood, approximately 3 × 3 in. for a base and about 2½ × 10 in. for the body. Drill a ⁹⁄₆₄-in. hole, about an inch from the top of the dummy body, through the center of the width and also through the center of the thickness. This way it can be used for any of the whirligigs. Cut the ⅛-in. rod to 3½ in.

Apply a drop of hot glue on the drilled hole, then push the ⅛-in. rod into the hole. Put the axle through the dummy and then put another drop of glue on the other paddle. Push the paddle onto the axle, with one paddle up, one paddle down so that the shoulders form a straight line with each other. Now test the movement of the paddles with a fan (even the fan from an air conditioner compressor works for this) or with the wind, if there is more than a slight breeze. If the paddles are perfectly balanced they will remain in a horizontal position when resting.

Painting. Once you are satisfied with the paddles it is time to paint your soldier. Mix the approximate recommended proportions and paint as follows:
Pants, paddles, cross strap: ¾ tsp. white/drop of burnt umber
Jacket, paddle tips: ½ tsp. red
Boots, hat: ½ tsp. mars black
Hair, brows, moustache: ½ tsp. raw umber
Face and ⅜-in. base: water down a drop of raw umber and paint with this "wash." Paint two other base pieces black.

When dry, spray with a protective semigloss lacquer.

Assembling. Hammer in brass pins where indicated on uniform.

To attach the paddles, first check to see if any hot glue remains in the arm holes; if so redrill the hole very carefully and the drill bit will pull out the dried glue. Mix the epoxy and put some of this in the axle hole of the paddle. Insert the 3½-in axle through the shoulders and put epoxy on each end of the axle. Do not use too much or you may end up with a paddle glued to the soldier. Press the first paddle on, then lay the soldier on his back. Push the other paddle on so that one paddle is up and the other down. Rest something under the paddles, if necessary, to keep them lined up straight. Let them dry completely.

Glue the small base piece on top of the large base piece. Cut ³⁄₁₆-in. metal rod with cutters to length desired and sand one end to a dull point with emery cloth. Insert the flat end of the rod into the base. Put the ⅜-in. base on the rod and then place the soldier on top. Glue the base to the bottom of the whirligig. If you have chosen to put your whirligig outdoors, simply put him and the ⅜-in. base on the rod and he's ready to whirl!

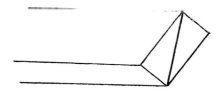

Illus. 17. Angle line for sanding, finished paddle

Policeman

MATERIALS

Pine, ¾ in. thick: 9 × 11 in.
Metal rod, ⅛ in. diameter: 2¼ in. long
Metal rod, 3/16 in. diameter: 2¼ in. long if to be mounted on base or 15 to 36-in. if not
Acrylic paint: titanium white, burnt umber, cerulean blue hue, mars black, naphthol red light
Permanent black marker

Illus. 18.

Brass escutcheon pins, ½ in. × 18: three
Sandpaper: medium and fine grades
Emery cloth
Epoxy glue
Semi-gloss lacquer spray
Tracing paper
Poster board

TOOLS

Scroll saw or band saw
Drill with ⅛, 9/64, 7/32, 3/16 in. bits
Stationary belt sander or sanding wheel: with medium-grade sandpaper
Metal cutters
Hot glue gun (optional): for testing paddles on dummy

INSTRUCTIONS

Pattern. Trace all pattern pieces and transfer onto poster board. Cut out templates, cutting outlines only. Trace all pattern pieces onto the ¾-in. pine board.

Cutting. Cut out all pieces with the saw and then cut out a 3½-in. × 3½-in. base.

Drilling. Drill into the shoulder area of the paddles as indicated using the ⅛-in. drill bit. Drill as straight and centered as possible, using a drill press if one is available. Drill a 9/64-in. hole through the shoulder area of the policeman, as marked on the pattern. Next, drill a 7/32-in. hole into the bottom of the policeman, as shown on the pattern. Finally, drill a 3/16-in. hole into the center of the base. Cut off the top ⅜ in. of a flathead nail or tack with metal cutters and insert this, flat side out, into the hole on the underside of the policeman. Tap this in with a dowel,

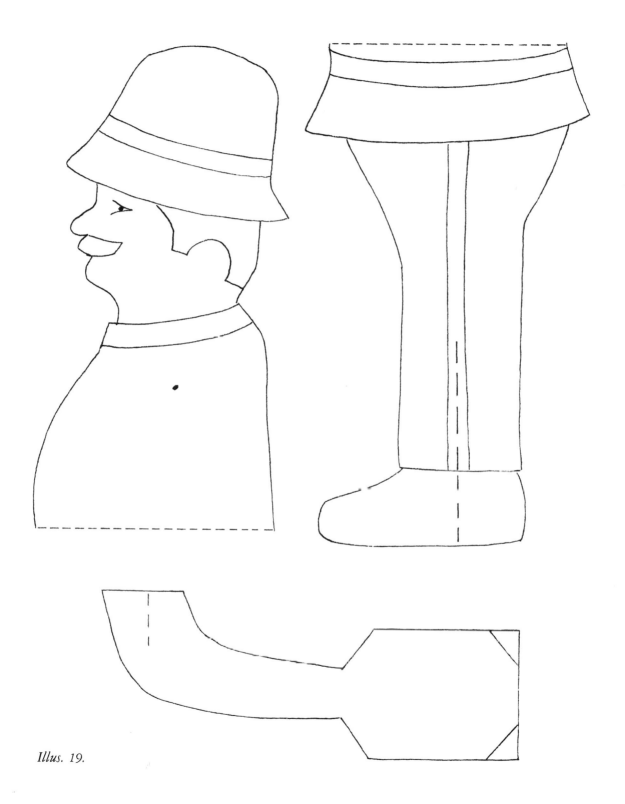

Illus. 19.

using a hammer if necessary (Illus. 13, p. 17).

Shaping Paddles. To form the paddles of the policeman first draw a diagonal line with a pencil from the top right corner to the bottom left corner on the end of each paddle. Hold the paddles side by side and make sure the paddles and angle lines are identical. It should appear that you are making two right paddles; however, when placed on the other side the paddle will be reversed, as it should be.

Always paying attention to the drawn pencil angle, take the paddle in your hand and gently press it against the sander. Keep the pencil line *parallel* to the sander at all times. Move the paddle back and forth against the sander. After you have sanded a portion away on one side, turn the paddle over and start sanding on the other side. Keep sanding both sides until you reduce the paddle (not the shoulders) to approximately ⅛ to ³⁄₁₆ in. It is very important to keep checking the angle (Illus. 42). This is why I prefer the sanding wheel, as I can see the angle more easily. Repeat this procedure with the other paddle, making them as identical as possible. Carefully cut off a small triangle from both bottom corners of each paddle. (Illus. 16A)

Sanding. Round the shoulder and arm of the paddles as much as possible with the sander. Also round the body edges, holding the edges at an angle to the sander to achieve a carved appearance. Sand the base piece. Give each piece a final sanding by hand with fine sandpaper.

Testing. Make a "dummy" whirligig out of ¾-in. scraps of wood, approximately 3 × 3-in. for a base, and about 2½ × 10-in. for the body. Drill a ⁹⁄₆₄-in. hole, about an inch from the top of the dummy body, through the center of the width and also through the center of the thickness. This way it can be used for any of the whirligigs. Cut the ⅛-in. rod to 2¼ in.

Apply a drop of hot glue on the drilled hole, then push the ⅛-in. rod into the hole. Put the axle through the dummy and put another drop of glue on the other paddle. Push the paddle onto the axle, with one paddle up, one paddle down so that the shoulders form a straight line with each other. Now test the movement of the paddles with a fan (even the fan from an air conditioner compressor works for this) or with the wind if there is more than a slight breeze. If the paddles are perfectly balanced they will remain in a horizontal position when resting.

Painting. Paint the policeman according to the proportions listed. These are approximations. Always start painting light areas first and end with the darkest.
Trim: ¼ tsp. white/drop of burnt umber
Uniform: ½ tsp. blue/drop of white/drop of black
Paddles: ⅛ tsp. red/few drops of black
Hair, moustache: ⅛ tsp. burnt umber/drop of red
Hat, shoes: ⅛ tsp. black
Base: ¼ tsp. white/drop of burnt umber
Skin: leave natural wood color

When dry, spray all pieces with a protective coating of semi-gloss lacquer spray. Draw an eye with a permanent black marker after the lacquer has dried.

Assembling. Hammer the three brass pins into the very front of the policeman's jacket. To attach paddles, first check to see if any hot glue remains in the arm holes; if so, redrill the hole very carefully and the drill bit will pull out the dried glue. Mix the epoxy and put some of this in the axle hole of the paddle. Insert the axle through the shoulders and put epoxy on each end of the axle. Do not use too much or you may end up with a paddle glued to your policeman. Press the first paddle on, then lay the policeman on his back. Push the other paddle on so that one paddle is up and the other down. Rest something under the paddles, if necessary, to keep them lined up straight. Let it dry completely.

Cut the $\frac{3}{16}$-in. metal rod with cutters to desired length and sand one end to a dull point with emery cloth. Insert the pointed end into the underside of the policeman. Either insert the other end into the base, if you are using your whirligig indoors as folk art, or put him outside to whirl in the wind.

...m

...RIALS

...e, ¾ in. thick; 6½ × 14 in.

Wood 2 × 4: 4½ in. long

Metal rod, ⅛ in. diameter: 4½ in. long

Metal rod, 3/16 in. diameter: 7 in. long if to be mounted on base or 15 to 36 in. long if not

Illus. 20.

Acrylic paint: titanium white, burnt umber, naphthol red light, mars black, cerulean blue hue

Brushes: ½ in. and ¼ in.

Sandpaper: medium and fine grades

Emery cloth

Epoxy glue

Semi-gloss lacquer spray

Tracing paper

Poster board

Permanent, black, fine-tip marker

TOOLS

Scroll saw or band saw

Drill with ⅛, 9/64, 3/16, and 7/32-in. bits

Extra length 7/32-in. drill bit (If not available, use an extra length 3/16-in. bit)

Stationary belt sander or sanding wheel and medium-grade sandpaper

Metal cutters

Hot glue gun (optional): for testing paddles on dummy

INSTRUCTIONS

Pattern. Trace both pattern pieces for Uncle Sam and transfer onto poster board. Cut out templates, cutting around outlines only. Trace pattern pieces onto ¾-in. wood, tracing two paddles.

Cutting. Cut out all pieces with the saw and then cut a 4½-in. length of 2 × 4 lumber.

Drilling. Use the ⅛-in. drill bit to drill a hole into the center shoulder area of the paddles as indicated. Drill as straight as possible, using a drill press if one is available. Paddles will not turn properly if the holes are crooked since everything will be

Illus. 21.

Arm and paddle pattern on next page

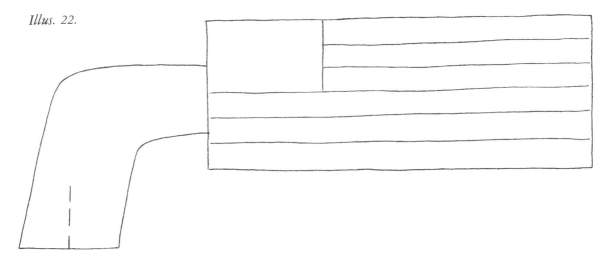

Illus. 22.

thrown off balance. Drill a %4-in. hole through the shoulder area of Uncle Sam as marked on the pattern. Next, drill a 7⁄32-in. hole with the extended drill bit up through the leg area. Final drilling is done with a 3⁄16-in. bit into the center of the 2 × 4 base.

Cut off the top 3⁄8-in. of a flathead nail or tack with metal cutters and insert this, flat side out, into the hole between legs. Tap it in with a dowel, using a hammer if necessary (Illus. 13, p. 17).

Shaping Paddles. To form Uncle Sam's paddles first draw an angle line with a pencil from the top right corner to the bottom left corner on the end of each paddle. Hold the paddles side by side and make sure the paddles and angle lines are identical. It needs to appear that you are making two right arms/paddles; however, when placed on the other side the arm will be reversed as it should be.

Always paying attention to the drawn pencil angle, take the paddle in your hand and gently press it against the sander. Keep the pencil line *parallel* to the sander at all times. Move the paddle back and forth against the sander. After you have sanded a portion away on one side turn the paddle over and start sanding on the other side. Keep sanding both sides until you reduce the paddle (not the shoulders) to approximately 1⁄8 to 3⁄16 in. It is very important to keep checking the angle (Illus. 17). This is why I prefer the sanding wheel as I can see the angle more easily. Repeat this procedure with the other paddle, making them as identical as possible.

Sanding. Round the shoulder and arm of the paddle as much as possible with the sander. Keep the side of the paddle that will be against the body as flat as possible; do not round these edges. Sand the body edges, holding them at an angle to the sander to achieve a carved appearance. Sand the base and then give each piece a final sanding by hand with fine sandpaper.

Testing. Make a "dummy" whirligig out of ¾-in. scraps of wood, approximately 3 × 3-in. for a base and about 2½ × 10-in. for the body. Drill a %₄-in. hole about an inch from the top of the dummy body through the center of the width and also through the center of the thickness. This way it can be used for any of the whirligigs. Cut the ⅛-in. rod to 4½ in.

Apply a drop of hot glue on the drilled hole, then push the ⅛-in. rod into the hole. Put the axle through the dummy and then put another drop of glue on the other paddle. Push the paddle onto the axle, with one paddle up, one paddle down, so that the shoulders form a straight line with each other. Now test the movement of the paddles with a fan (even the fan from an air conditioner compressor works for this) or with the wind, if there is more than a slight breeze. If the paddles are perfectly balanced they will remain in a horizontal position when resting.

Painting. Paint Uncle Sam with paints listed. Measurements are approximate. Always start with lightest colors, ending with darkest.
Beard, white stripes: ¾ tsp. white/drop of burnt umber
Vest, red stripes: ¾ tsp. red/drop of black
Jacket, brim: ¼ tsp. blue/few drops of black/few drops of white
Face: ⅛ tsp. white/drop of red/drop of burnt umber
Buttons (last): drop of white

After the paint has dried spray each piece with a protective coat of semi-gloss lacquer. When it is dry, draw the eyes with permanent, black, fine-tip marker.

Assembling. To attach Uncle Sam's flag paddles, first check to see if any hot glue remains in the paddle holes; if so, redrill the hole very carefully and the drill bit will pull out the dried glue. Mix epoxy and put some of this in the axle hole of the paddle. Insert the axle through the shoulders and put epoxy on each end of the axle. Do not use too much or you may end up with a paddle glued to Uncle Sam. Press the first paddle on, then lay Uncle Sam on his back. Push the other paddle on so that one paddle is up and the other down. Rest something under the paddles, if necessary, to keep them lined up straight. Let them dry completely.

Cut the ³⁄₁₆-in. metal rod to the desired length with cutters, depending on whether you are using a base or not. Sand one end to a dull point with emery cloth. Insert this end into Uncle Sam, place him on the base or outdoors, and he's ready to wave Old Glory.

Illus. 23.

Pirate

MATERIALS

Pine, ¾ in. thick: 5½ × 10 in.

Pine, ¾ in. thick (optional 2-tier base): 5 × 8 in.

Wooden dowel, ⅜ in. diameter: 1⅜ in. long for peg leg

Metal rod, ⅛ in. diameter: 4 in. long

Metal rod, 3⁄16 in. diameter: 4 in. long if to be mounted on base or 15 to 36 in. if not

Acrylic paint: titanium white, burnt umber, naphthol red light, mars black, raw umber

Brushes: ½ in., ¼ in.

Semi-gloss lacquer spray

Sandpaper: medium and fine grades

Emery cloth

Wood glue

Epoxy glue

Tracing paper

Poster board

TOOLS

Scroll saw or band saw

Drill with ⅛, 9⁄64, 7⁄32, and 3⁄16-in. bits

Stationary belt sander or sanding wheel and medium-grade sandpaper

Metal cutters

Hot glue gun (optional): for testing paddles on dummy

INSTRUCTIONS

Pattern. Trace pattern pieces for the pirate and transfer onto poster board. Cut out templates, cutting around the outlines only. Trace these pattern pieces onto the ¾-in. wood.

Cutting. Cut out the pieces for the pirate

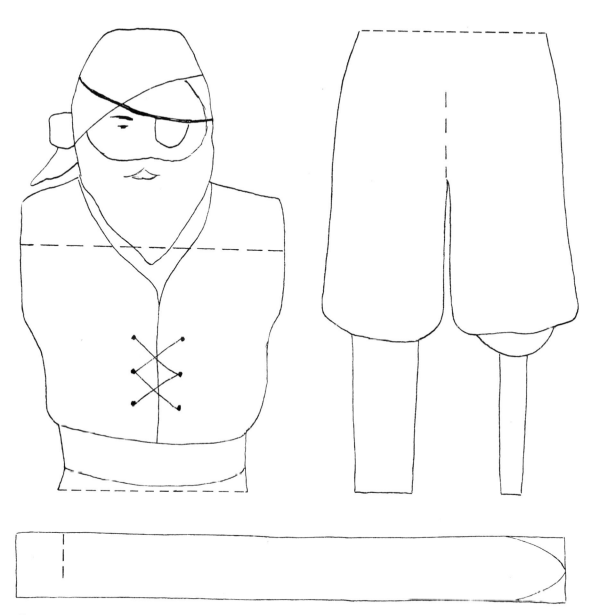

Illus. 24A.

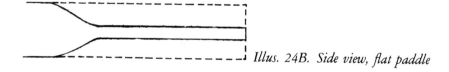

Illus. 24B. Side view, flat paddle

and then cut two base pieces, 3 × 3-in. and 4½ × 4½-in. Also cut the ⅜-in.-diameter dowel to a length of 1⅜-in.

Drilling. Drill a ⅛-in.-diameter hole into the shoulder area of the paddles, as indicated. Drill as straight as possible, using a drill press if one is available. Use a %₆₄-in. bit to drill a hole through the shoulder area of the pirate, as marked on the pattern. Next, drill a ⁷⁄₃₂-in. hole into the bottom of the pirate between the legs. Final drilling is done with a ³⁄₁₆-in. bit through the center of the small 3 × 3-in. base.

Cut off the top ⅜ in. flat head of a tack or nail with metal cutters and insert this, flat side out, into the hole between the legs of the pirate. Tap this in with a dowel, using a hammer if necessary (Illus. 13, p. 17).

Shaping Paddles. This is the only whirligig in this book with solid paddles that are not sanded at an angle. For the pirate you need to sand one paddle so that the flat side faces frontward and the other paddle should be sanded to have the flat side face sideward. Sand all but the last 1¾ in. at the shoulder into a flat paddle (Illus. 24).

Start by taking the paddle in your hand and gently pressing it against the sander. Move the paddle back and forth against the sander. After you have sanded a portion away on one side, turn the paddle over and start sanding on the other side. Keep the paddle *parallel* to the sander at all times. Sand both sides until you reduce the paddle to approximately ⅛ to ³⁄₁₆

in. (Illus. 17). Repeat this procedure with the other paddle; however, be sure to make one paddle facing the front and the other facing the side. Sand the tips to a tapered point.

Sanding. Using the sander, round the shoulder and arm of the paddles as much as possible. Also round the body edges, holding the edges at an angle to the sander to achieve a carved appearance. Sand all base pieces. Round the ⅜-in. dowel to a tapered peg shape. Give each piece a final sanding by hand with fine sandpaper.

Testing. Make a "dummy" whirligig out of ¾-in. scraps of wood, approximately 3 × 3-in. for a base and about 2½ × 10-in. for the body. Drill a %₆₄-in. hole, about an inch from the top of the dummy body, through the center of the width and also through the center of the thickness. This way it can be used for any of the whirligigs. Cut the ⅛-in. rod to 4 in.

Apply a drop of hot glue on the drilled hole, then push the ⅛-in. rod into the hole. Put the axle through the dummy and then put another drop of glue on the other paddle. Push the paddle onto the axle, with one paddle up, one paddle down, so that the shoulders form a straight line with each other. Now test the movement of the paddles with a fan (even the fan from an air conditioner compressor works for this) or with the wind, if there is more than a slight breeze.

Painting. Paint the pirate using the following paints. Measurements are approximate. Paint lightest areas first, ending with darkest.

Shirt: ½ tsp. white/drop of burnt umber
Scarf, belt: ¼ tsp. red/drop of black
Beard: ⅛ tsp. burnt umber/drop of red
Pants, eyepatch: ½ tsp. black
Top base: ¼ tsp. red/drop of black
Bottom base: ¼ tsp. black
Face, paddles, leg: ⅛ tsp. raw umber; mix with about ½ tsp. water and paint with this "wash"
Peg leg: Paint with a slightly darker raw umber "wash"

Assembling: To attach the paddles, first check to see if any hot glue remains in the arm holes; if so, redrill the hole very carefully and the drill bit will pull out the dried glue. Mix epoxy and put some of this in the axle hole of the paddle. Insert the axle through the shoulders and put epoxy on each end of the axle. Do not use too much or you may end up with a paddle glued to the pirate. Press the first paddle on, then lay him on his back. Push the other paddle on so that one paddle is up and the other down. Rest something under the paddles, if necessary, to keep them lined up straight. Let them dry completely.

Glue the small base piece on top of the large base piece. Cut the ³⁄₁₆-in. metal rod with cutters to the length desired and sand one end to a dull point with emery cloth. Place the pirate on the rod and then set into the base, or if your pirate will be outdoors, place him on a longer rod and position outside where he can gallantly battle the wind.

Sailor

MATERIALS

Pine, ¾ in. thick: 10 × 12 in.
Metal rod, ⅛ in. diameter: 2¼ in. long
Metal rod, 3⁄16 in. diameter: 3 in. long if to
be mounted on base or 15 to 36 in. if not
Acrylic paint: titanium white, cerulean
blue hue, mars black
Stain: medium color
Semi-gloss lacquer spray
Sandpaper: medium and fine grades
Emery cloth

Illus. 25.

Brushes: ½ in. and ¼ in.
Epoxy glue
Tracing paper
Poster board

TOOLS

Scroll saw or band saw
Drill with ⅛, 9⁄64, 3⁄16, and 7⁄32-in. bits
Stationary belt sander or sanding wheel:
with medium-grade sandpaper
Metal cutters
Hot glue gun (optional): for testing pad-
dles on dummy

INSTRUCTIONS

Pattern. Trace pattern pieces and transfer
onto poster board, including all paint
lines. Cut out templates, cutting outline
only. Trace pattern of sailor and two paddles onto ¾-in. pine.

Cutting. From ¾-in. wood, cut all pieces,
including a 4 × 4-in. square for the base.

Drilling. Drill a ⅛-in.-diameter hole
into the shoulder part of the paddles as
marked. All holes must be as straight as
possible. I suggest the use of a drill press,
if you have access to one. Using the 9⁄64-in.
drill bit, drill a hole for the axle through
the body of the sailor as marked. Remember, these holes are critical for balancing
the paddles. Drill a hole with the 7⁄32-in.
bit into the bottom on the sailor. Then,
using the 3⁄16-in. bit, drill a hole in the
center of the base. Cut off the top ⅜-in.
flat head of a tack or nail with metal cutters and insert this, flat side out, into the
bottom of the sailor. Tap it in with a
dowel (Illus. 13, p. 17).

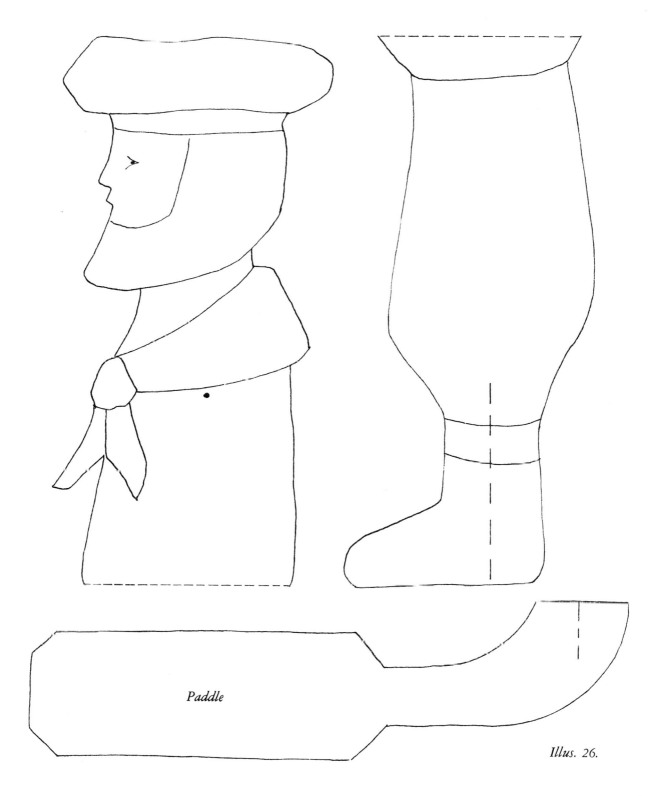

Paddle

Illus. 26.

Shaping Paddles. To shape the sailor's paddles first draw an angle line with a pencil from the top right corner to the bottom left corner on the end of each paddle. Hold the paddles side by side and make sure the paddles and angle lines are identical. It must appear that you are making two right arms/paddles; however, when placed on the other side the arm will be reversed as it should be.

Always paying attention to the drawn pencil angle, take the paddle in your hand and gently press it against the sander. Keep the pencil line *parallel* to the sander at all times. Move the paddle back and forth against the sander. After you have sanded a portion away on one side, turn the paddle over and start sanding on the other side. Keep sanding both sides until you reduce the paddle to approximately ⅛ to 3/16 in. (Illus. 17). It is very important to keep checking the angle. This is why I prefer the sanding wheel, as I can see the angle more easily. Repeat this procedure with the other paddle, making them as identical as possible.

Sanding. Round the shoulder and arm of the paddles as much as possible using the sander. Also round the body edges, holding the edges at an angle to the sander to achieve a carved appearance. Sand the base piece. Give each piece a final sanding by hand with fine sandpaper.

Testing. Make a "dummy" whirligig out of ¾-in. scraps of wood, approximately 3 × 3-in. for a base and about 2½ × 10-in. for the body. Drill a 9/64-in. hole, about an inch from the top of the dummy body,

through the center of the width and also through the center of the thickness. This way it can be used for any of the whirligigs. Cut the ⅛-in. rod to 2¼ in.

Apply a drop of hot glue on the drilled hole, then push the ⅛-in. rod into the hole. Put the axle through the dummy and then put another drop of glue on the other paddles. Push the paddle onto the axle, with one paddle up, one paddle down so that the shoulders form a straight line with each other. Now test the movement of the paddles with a fan (even the fan from an air conditioner compressor works for this) or with the wind, if there is more than a slight breeze. If the paddles are perfectly balanced they will remain in a horizontal position when resting.

Painting. Paint the sailor by mixing the paints below. Remember to paint the light colors first, ending with the darkest.
Hat, shirt, socks: ½ tsp. white
Pants, sleeves, collar: ½ tsp. blue/drop of white/drop of black
Base, boots, beard, moustache, eyes: 1 tsp. black

Staining. Apply a light coat of medium-color stain with a cloth to paddles and entire sailor body. Wipe off excess and let it dry. When it is dry, spray a protective coat of semi-gloss lacquer over each piece. Be sure to check compatibility with the stain first.

Assembling. To attach the paddles, first check to see if any hot glue remains in the arm holes; if so, redrill the hole very carefully and the drill bit will pull out the dried glue. Mix the epoxy and put some of it in the axle hole of the paddle. Insert the axle through the shoulders and put epoxy on each end of the axle. Do not use too much or you may end up with a paddle glued to the sailor. Press the first paddle on, then lay the sailor on his back. Push the other paddle on so that one paddle is up and the other down. Rest something under the paddles, if necessary, to keep them lined up straight. Let the glue dry completely.

Cut the ³⁄₁₆-in. metal rod with cutters to desired length and sand one end to a dull point with emery cloth. Insert this end into the bottom of the sailor. If you are using a base, insert the other end into it. If your sailor is going outdoors, simply put him on the metal rod and he's ready to sail!

Indian in Canoe

MATERIALS

Pine, ¾ in. thick: 6½ × 12 in.
Pine, ¾ in. thick (optional 3-tier base): 6 × 8 in.
Metal rod, ⅛ in. diameter: 2¼ in. long

Metal rod, ³⁄₁₆ in. diameter: 4 in. long if to be mounted on a base or 15 to 20 in. long if not
Acrylic paint: permanent green deep, mars black, naphthol red light, turner's yellow, burnt umber .
Stain: medium color
Semi-gloss lacquer spray

Illus. 27.

Sandpaper: medium and fine grades
Emery cloth
Wood glue
Epoxy glue
Tracing paper
Poster board

TOOLS

Scroll saw or band saw
Drill with ⅛, ⁹⁄₆₄, ⁷⁄₃₂, ³⁄₁₆-in. bits
Stationary belt sander or sanding wheel:
with medium-grade sandpaper
Metal cutters
Hot glue gun (optional): for testing paddles on dummy

INSTRUCTIONS

Pattern. Trace both pattern pieces for the Indian and transfer onto poster board. Cut out templates, cutting around the outline only. Trace pattern pieces for one Indian and two paddles onto the pine board.

Cutting. Cut out all three pieces for the Indian whirligig. Then cut out three base pieces: 2 × 2½ in., 2 × 4 in. and 3½ × 7½ in.

Drilling. Drill a ⅛-in.-diameter hole into the shoulder area of each paddle. Drill as straight as possible, using a drill press if available. Then, using the ⁹⁄₆₄-in. bit, drill a hole through the shoulder area of the Indian as marked. Next, drill a ⁷⁄₃₂-in. hole into the bottom of the canoe, as indicated on the pattern. Finally, drill a ³⁄₁₆-in. hole into the center of the 2 × 2½-in. base piece.

Cut off the top ⅜ in. of a flathead nail or tack with metal cutters and insert it, flat side out, into the hole on the underside of the canoe. Tap it in with a dowel, using a hammer if necessary (Illus. 13, p. 17).

Shaping Paddles. To form the paddles for the Indian first draw an angle line with a pencil from the top right corner to the bottom left corner on the end of each paddle. Hold the paddles side by side and make sure the paddles and angle lines are identical. It should appear that you are making two right arms/paddles; however, when placed on the other side the arm will be reversed as it should be. With these paddles you may take a shortcut, using the band saw, to remove some of the excess wood from the paddle (see p. 12, General Instructions) and then proceed with the sanding as described here, or you may do the entire shaping with the sander.

Always paying attention to the drawn pencil angle, take the paddle in your hand and gently press it against the sander. Keep the pencil line *parallel* to the sander at all times. Move the paddle back and forth against the sander. After you have sanded a portion away on one side turn the paddle over and start sanding on the other side. Keep sanding both sides until you reduce the paddle (not the shoulders) to approximately ⅛ to ³⁄₁₆ in. (Illus. 17). It is very important to keep checking the angle. This is why I prefer the sanding wheel, as I can see the angle easier. Repeat this procedure with the other paddle, making them as identical as possible.

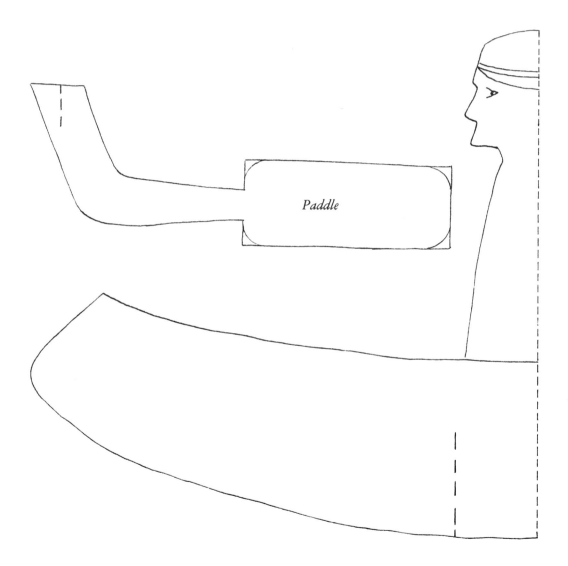

Paddle

Illus. 28.

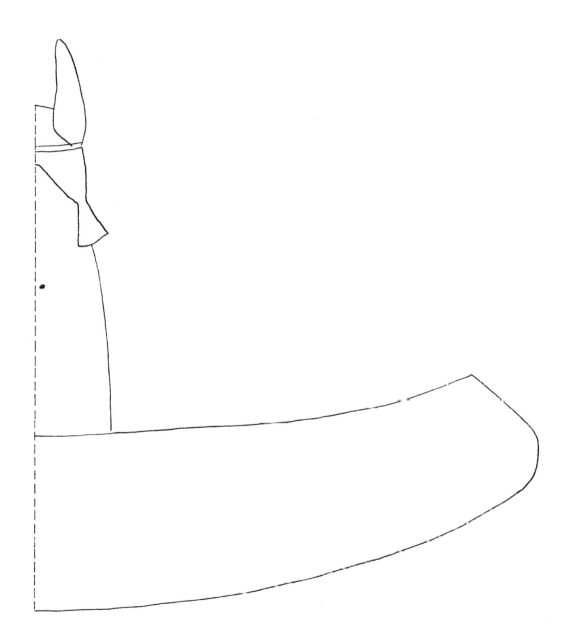

Sanding. Round the shoulder and arm of the paddles as much as possible with the sander. Keep the side of the paddle that will be against the body as flat as possible; do not round these edges. Also round the body edges, holding the edges at an angle to the sander to achieve a carved appearance. Sand all base pieces. Give each piece a final sanding by hand with fine sandpaper.

Testing. Make a "dummy" whirligig out of ¾-in. scraps of wood, approximately 3 × 3 in. for a base and about 2½ × 10 in. for the body. Drill a ⁹⁄₆₄-in. hole, about an inch from the top of the dummy body, through the center of the width and also through the center of the thickness. This way it can be used for any of the whirligigs. Cut the ⅛-in. rod to 2¼ in.

Apply a drop of hot glue on the drilled hole, then push the ⅛-in. rod into the hole. Put the axle through the dummy and then put another drop of glue on the other paddle. Push the paddle onto the axle, with one paddle up, one paddle down so that the shoulders form a straight line with each other. Now test the movement of the paddles with a fan (even the fan from an air conditioner compressor works for this) or with the wind, if there is more than a slight breeze. If the paddles are perfectly balanced they will remain in a horizontal position when resting.

Painting. Using the approximate proportions listed, paint the Indian and his canoe. Start with lightest colors first. Paddles: ⅛ tsp. yellow/drop of burnt umber

Canoe: ½ tsp. green/drop of black
Feather: drop of red
Hair, eyes: ⅛ tsp. black
Bases: ½ tsp. red/½ tsp. burnt umber

Staining. Using a cloth, wipe medium-color stain over the entire Indian, canoe, and paddles. Wipe off any excess. Let them dry and then spray with a protective coat of semi-gloss lacquer.

Assembling. Glue the base pieces together, one on top of the other. To attach the paddles of the Indian, first check to see if any hot glue remains in the arm holes; if so, redrill the holes of the paddle very carefully and the drill bit will pull out the dried glue. Mix the epoxy and put some of this in the axle hole of the paddles. A toothpick is handy for this.

Insert the axle through the shoulder and put a small amount of epoxy on each end of the axle. Do not use too much or you may end up with a paddle glued to the Indian. Press the first paddle on, then prop the canoe in an upright position. Push the other paddle on so that one paddle is forward and the other back. Set a scrap of wood under the paddles while drying in order to keep the shoulders in a straight line. Let the glue dry completely.

Cut the ³⁄₁₆-in. metal rod with cutters to desired length and sand one end to a dull point with emery cloth. Insert the pointed end into the underside of the canoe. Either insert the other end into the base, if you are using your whirligig indoors as folk art, or put him outside to paddle in the wind.

Mermaid

MATERIALS

Pine, ¾ in. thick: 11 × 15 in.
Wood base (optional)
    Pine, ¾ in. thick: 6½ × 7½ in.
    Finial (any shape): 3 in. diameter, 6 in.
    high
Metal rod, ⅛ in. diameter: 2¼ in. long
Metal rod, ³⁄₁₆ in. diameter: 8½ in. long if
to be mounted on a base or 15 to 36 in.
if not
Acrylic paint: cerulean blue hue, titanium
white, hooker's green, turner's yellow,
burnt umber
Stain: medium color
Brush: ½ in.
Sandpaper: medium and fine grades
Emery cloth

Illus. 29.

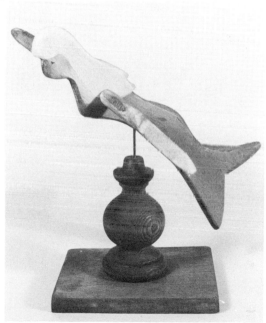

Epoxy glue
Wood glue
Tracing paper
Poster board
Semi-gloss lacquer spray
Permanent, black, fine-point marker

TOOLS

Scroll saw or band saw
Drill with ⅛, ⁹⁄₆₄, ³⁄₁₆, and ⁷⁄₃₂-in. bits
Stationary belt sander or sanding wheel:
with medium-grade sandpaper
Metal cutters
Hot glue gun (optional): for testing pad-
dles on dummy

INSTRUCTIONS

Pattern. Trace the pattern pieces and
transfer them onto poster board, including paint lines. Cut out templates, cutting
outline only. Trace pattern for mermaid
and two paddles onto ¾-in. pine.

Cutting. Cut mermaid body and paddle
arms with the saw. Also cut a 6½ × 7½-
in. base piece.

Drilling. Drill a ⅛-in. hole into the
shoulder area of the paddles, as marked.
Since all holes must be drilled as straight
as possible, use a drill press if one is available. Drill a hole for the axle through the
body of the mermaid where indicated
with the ⁹⁄₆₄-in. bit. Using the ⁷⁄₃₂-in bit,
drill up through the bottom of the mermaid at the angle on the pattern. Then
drill a ³⁄₁₆-in. hole into the finial if you
plan to use a base. Cut off the top ⅜ in.
flat head of a tack or nail with metal cutters and insert it, flat side out, into the
hole on the underside of the mermaid.

Paddle

Illus. 30.

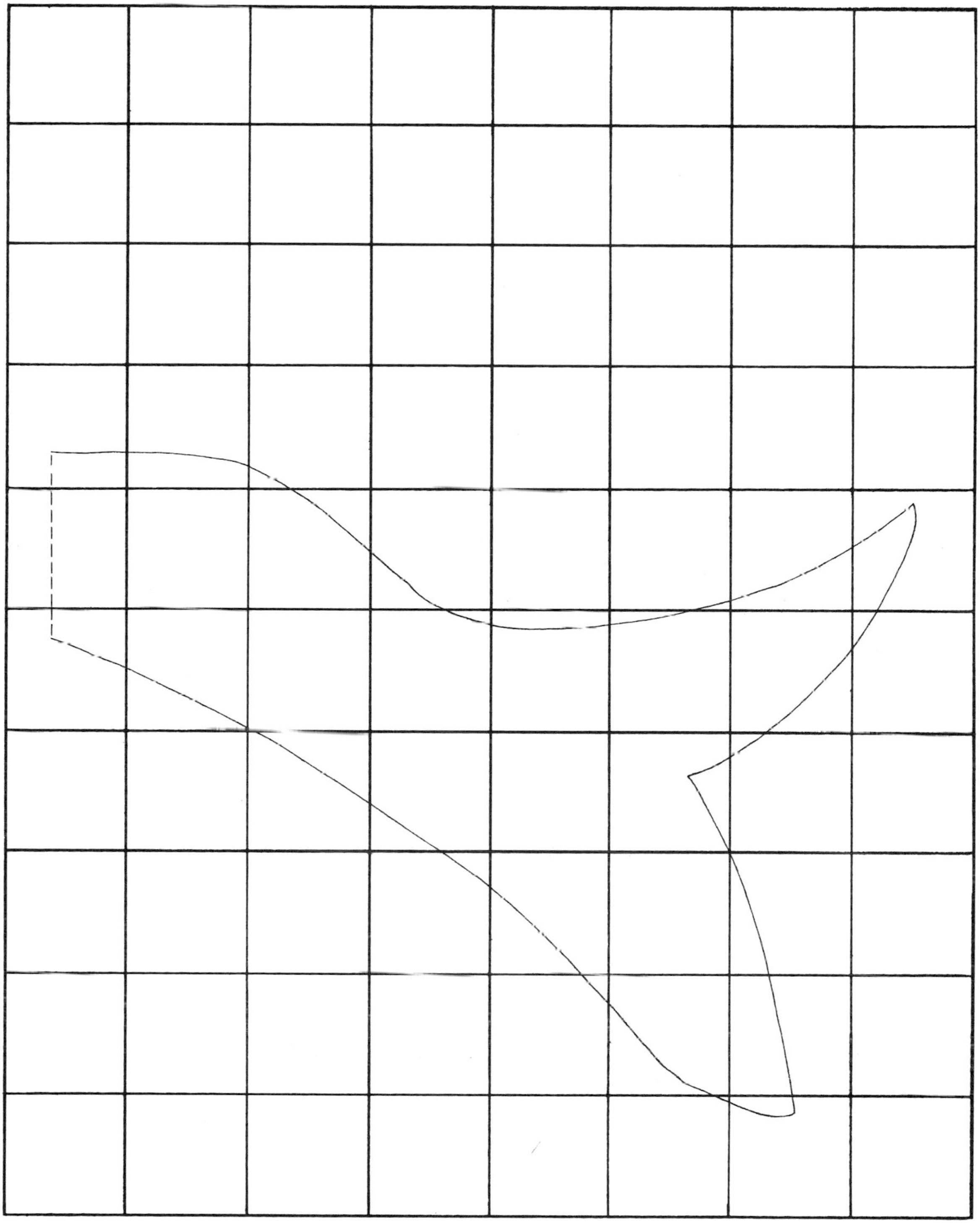

Tap in with a dowel, using a hammer if necessary (Illus. 13, p. 17).

Shaping Paddles. To form the paddles of the mermaid first draw an angle line with a pencil from the top right corner to the bottom left corner on the end of each paddle. Hold the paddles side by side and make sure the paddles and angle lines are identical. It should appear that you are making two right arms/paddles; however, when placed on the other side the arm will be reversed as it should be.

Always paying attention to the drawn pencil angle, take the paddle in your hand and gently press it against the sander. Keep the pencil line *parallel* to the sander at all times. Move the paddle back and forth against the sander. After you have sanded a portion away on one side, turn the paddle over and start sanding on the other side. Keep sanding both sides until you reduce the paddle (not the shoulders) to approximately ⅛ to 3/16 in. It is very important to keep checking the angle. This is why I prefer the sanding wheel, as I can see the angle more easily. Repeat this procedure with the other paddle, making them as identical as possible.

Sanding. Round the shoulder and arm of the paddles as much as possible with the sander. Keep the side of the paddle that will be against the body as flat as possible. Do not round these edges. Round the body edges, holding the edges at an angle to the sander to achieve a carved appearance. Sand all base pieces. Give each piece a final sanding by hand with fine sandpaper.

Testing. Make a "dummy" whirligig out of ¾-in. scraps of wood, approximately 3 × 3 in. for a base and about 2½ × 10 in. for the body. Drill a 9/64-in. hole about an inch from the top of the dummy body, through the center of the width and also through the center of the thickness. This way it can be used for any of the whirligigs. Cut the ⅛ in. rod to 2¼ in.

Apply a drop of hot glue on the drilled hole, then push the ⅛-in. rod into the hole. Push the axle through the dummy and then put another drop of glue on the other paddle. Push the paddle onto the axle, with one paddle up, one paddle down so that the shoulders form a straight line with each other. Now test the movement of the paddles with a fan (even the fan from an air conditioner compressor works for this) or with the wind, if there is more than a slight breeze. If the paddles are perfectly balanced they will remain in a horizontal position when resting.

Painting. Paint the mermaid, using the approximate proportions given.
Hair: ¼ tsp. turner's yellow/drop of burnt umber
Mermaid: ½ tsp. white/½ tsp. blue/few drops of green

Staining. Apply a medium-color stain to the entire mermaid and paddles and let it dry. Spray all pieces with a protective coat of semi-gloss lacquer. After it has dried, draw eyes with the permanent marker.

Assembling. To attach the mermaid's

paddles, first check to see if any hot glue remains in the arm holes; if so, redrill the hole very carefully and the drill bit will pull out the dried glue. Mix epoxy and put some of this in the axle hole of the paddle. Insert the axle through the shoulders and put epoxy on each end of the axle. Do not use too much or you may end up with a paddle glued to your mermaid. Press the first paddle on, then lay the mermaid on her back. Push the other paddle on so that one paddle is up and the other down. Rest something under the paddles, if necessary, to keep them lined up straight. Let them dry completely.

Cut the ³⁄₁₆-in. metal rod with cutters to the desired length, which depends on whether you use a base or not. Sand one end to a dull point with emery cloth. Insert this end into the mermaid and then place her on the base or outdoors to swim in the breeze.

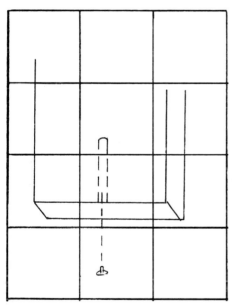

Illus. 31. Inserting flathead tack

Fisherman

MATERIALS

Pine, ¾ in. thick: 8 × 14 in.
Metal rod, ⅛ in. diameter: 3⅞ in. long
Metal rod, 3/16 in. diameter: 5 in. long if it will be mounted on a base or 15 to 36 in. long if not
Acrylic paint: titanium white, raw umber, mars black, naphthol red light, chromium oxide green
Brushes: ½ in., ¼ in., and 1/16 in. round

Sandpaper: medium and fine grades
Emery cloth
Epoxy glue
Semi-gloss lacquer spray
Tracing paper
Poster board

TOOLS

Scroll saw or band saw
Drill with ⅛, 9/64, 7/32, and 3/16-in. bits
Extended length drill bit: 7/32 in. (if not available, use extended 3/16 in.)
Stationary belt sander or sanding wheel: with medium-grade sandpaper
Metal cutters
Hot glue gun (optional): for testing paddles on dummy

INSTRUCTIONS

Pattern. Trace both pattern pieces for the fisherman, including paint lines, then transfer onto poster board. Cut out templates, cutting around the outline only. Trace pattern pieces onto the ¾-in. wood.

Cutting. Cut out the fisherman's body and two paddles with the scroll or band saw. Cut a 2 × 3½-in. base.

Drilling. Drill a ⅛-in.-diameter hole into the shoulder area of the paddles as indicated. Drill all holes as straight as possible, using a drill press if available. Use a 9/64-in. bit to drill a hole through the shoulder section of the body. Next, drill a 7/32-in.-diameter hole, using the extended drill bit, up between the legs of the fisherman. If you will be using your whirligig outdoors, drill an additional 7/32-in.-diameter hole through the center of the base piece (the pivot rod will pass through the

Illus. 32.

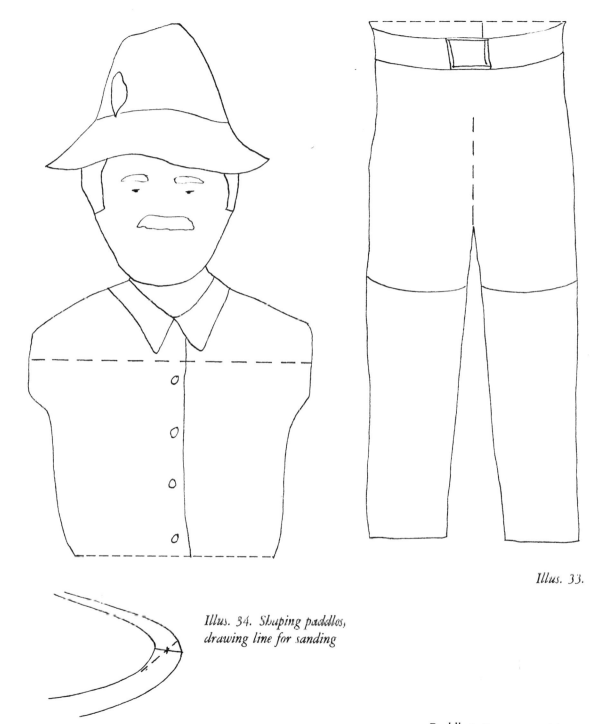

Illus. 33.

Illus. 34. Shaping paddles, drawing line for sanding

Paddle pattern on next page

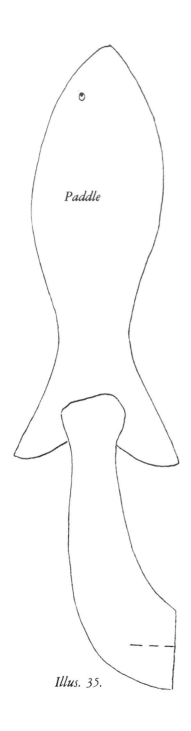

Paddle

Illus. 35.

base). If your fisherman will be adding a little whimsy indoors, drill a ³⁄₁₆-in.-diameter hole into the center of the base.

Cut off the top ³⁄₈ in. of the flat head of a tack or nail with metal cutters and insert this, flat side out, into the hole between the fisherman's legs. Tap this in with a dowel, using a hammer if necessary (Illus. 13, p. 17).

Shaping Paddles. To form the paddles of the fisherman first draw an angled line on the tip of the paddle (approximately 45° where the line meets the flat side). Since the paddle is curved at the end, this is done by first drawing a line at the tip of the paddle, from top to bottom and then marking the center of the line. Then draw equal lines on both sides of this line when drawing the 45° angle (Illus. 34). Lay the paddles side by side and make sure the paddles and angle lines are identical. It should appear that you are making two right paddles; however, when placed on the other side, the arm will be reversed as it should be.

Always paying attention to the drawn pencil angle, take the paddle in your hand and gently press it against the sander. Keep the pencil line *parallel* to the sander at all times. Move the paddle back and forth against the sander. After you have sanded a portion away on one side, turn the paddle over and start sanding on the other side. Keep sanding both sides until you reduce the paddle (not the shoulder) to approximately ⅛ to ³⁄₁₆ in. (Illus. 17). It is very important to keep checking the angle. This is why I prefer the sanding wheel, as I can see the angle more easily. Repeat this procedure with the other paddle, making them as identical as possible.

Sanding. Round the shoulder and arm of the paddles as much as possible with the sander. Keep the side of the paddle that will be against the body as flat as possible. Do not round these edges. Round the body edges, holding the edges at an angle to the sander to achieve a carved appearance. Sand the base piece. Give each piece a final sanding by hand with fine sandpaper.

Testing. Make a "dummy" whirligig out of ¾ in. scraps of wood, approximately 3 × 3 in. for a base and about 2½ × 10 in. for the body. Drill a %₄-in. hole about an inch from the top of the dummy body, through the center of the width, and also through the center of the thickness. This way it can be used for any of the whirligigs. Cut the ⅛-in. rod to 3⅞ in.

Apply a drop of hot glue on the drilled hole, then push the ⅛-in. rod into the hole. Put the axle through the dummy and then put another drop of glue on the other paddle. Push the paddle onto the axle, with one paddle up, one paddle down so that the shoulders form a straight line with each other. Now test the movement of the paddles with a fan (even the fan from an air conditioner compressor works for this) or with the wind, if there is more than a slight breeze. If the paddles are perfectly balanced they will remain in a horizontal position when resting.

Painting. To paint the fisherman, mix the proportions of paint listed. Measurements are approximate. Paint light areas first, ending with the darkest. Refer to the pattern for paint lines.
Shirt: ½ tsp. yellow/drop of raw umber
Hair, moustache, brows: ⅛ tsp. white/ ⅛ tsp. black
Fish: ¼ tsp. green/few drops of white
Base, hat, collar, trousers: ¼ tsp. raw umber
Belt, feather: ⅛ tsp. red
Hip boots: ⅛ tsp. black
Skin: ⅛ tsp. white, drop of red/drop of raw umber
Eyes: drop of black

Spray each piece with a protective coat of semi-gloss lacquer.

Assembling. To attach the fisherman's paddles, first check to see if any hot glue remains in the arm holes; if so, redrill the hole very carefully and the drill bit will pull out the dried glue. Mix the epoxy and put some of this in the axle hole of the paddle. Insert the axle through the shoulders and put epoxy on each end of the axle. Do not use too much or you may end up with a paddle glued to the fisherman. Press the first paddle on, then lay the fisherman on his back. Push the other paddle on so that one paddle is up and the other down. Rest something under the paddles, if necessary, to keep them lined up straight. Let them dry completely.

Glue the fisherman onto the base and let the glue dry. Then cut the ³⁄₁₆-in. metal rod with cutters to the desired length, depending on use. Sand one end to a dull point with emery cloth. Insert this end into the fisherman and then set him into the base or if he will be outdoors, position him where he can catch the most wind with his fish.

Penguin

MATERIALS

Pine, ¾ in. thick: 7 × 11 in.
Metal rod, ⅛ in. diameter: 2¼ in. long
Metal rod, ³⁄₁₆ in. diameter: 2½ in. long if it is to be mounted on a base or 15 to 20 in. if not
Acrylic paint: titanium white, mars black, turner's yellow, burnt umber, naphthol red light
Brush: ½ in., ¹⁄₁₆ in. round
Sandpaper: medium and fine grades
Emery cloth
Epoxy glue

Semi-gloss lacquer spray
Tracing paper
Poster board

TOOLS

Scroll or band saw
Drill with ⅛, ⁹⁄₆₄, ⁷⁄₃₂, and ³⁄₁₆-in. bits
Stationary belt sander or sanding wheel: with medium-grade sandpaper
Metal cutters
Hot glue gun (optional): for testing paddles on dummy

INSTRUCTIONS

Pattern. Trace both pattern pieces for the penguin and transfer onto poster board. Cut out templates, cutting around the outline only. Trace pattern for penguin body and two paddles onto the ¾-in wood.

Cutting. Cut out all the pieces with the saw and then cut a base, 3 × 3 in.

Drilling. Drill a ⅛-in.-diameter hole into the shoulder area of the paddles, as indicated. Drill as straight as possible, using a drill press if available. Use a ⁹⁄₆₄-in. bit to drill a hole through the shoulder area of the penguin, as marked on the pattern. Next drill a ⁷⁄₃₂-in.-diameter hole into the bottom of the penguin, between the legs. Final drilling is done with a ³⁄₁₆-in. bit through the center of the base.

With metal cutters, cut off the top ⅜ in. of the flat head of a tack or nail and insert this, flat side out, into the hole on the underside of the penguin. Tap this in with a dowel, using a hammer if necessary (Illus. 13, p. 17).

Shaping Paddles. To form the paddles of

Illus. 36.

59

Paddle

Illus. 37.

the penguin first draw an angled line on the tip of the paddle (approximately 45° where the line meets the flat side). Since the paddle is curved at the end, this is done by first drawing a line at the tip of the paddle, from top to bottom and then marking the center of the line. Then, draw equal lines on both sides of this line when drawing the 45° angle (Illus. 34, p. 35). Lay the paddles side by side and make sure the paddles and angle lines are identical. It should appear that you are making two right paddles; however, when placed on the other side, the arm will be reversed as it should be.

Always paying attention to the drawn pencil angle, take the paddle in your hand and gently press it against the sander. Keep the pencil line *parallel* to the sander at all times. Move the paddle back and forth against the sander. After you have sanded a portion away on one side, turn the paddle over and start sanding on the other side. Keep sanding both sides until you reduce the paddle (not the shoulder) to approximately 1/8 to 3/16 in. (Illus. 17). It is very important to keep checking the angle. This is why I prefer the sanding wheel, as I can see the angle more easily. Repeat this procedure with the other paddle, making them as identical as possible.

Sanding. Round the shoulder and arm of the paddles as much as possible with the sander. Keep the side of the paddle that will be against the body as flat as possible. Do not round these edges. Round the body edges, holding the edges at an angle to the sander to achieve a carved appearance. Sand the base piece. Give each piece

a final sanding by hand with fine sandpaper.

Testing. Make a "dummy" whirligig out of ¾-in. scraps of wood, approximately 3 × 3-in. for a base and about 2½ × 10-in. for the body. Drill a 9/64-in. hole about an inch from the top of the dummy body, through the center of the width and also through the center of the thickness. This way it can be used for any of the whirligigs. Cut the 1/8-in. rod to 2¼-in.

Apply a drop of hot glue on the drilled hole, then push the 1/8-in. rod into the hole. Put the axle through the dummy and then put another drop of glue on the other paddle. Push the paddle onto the axle, with one paddle up, one paddle down so that the shoulders form a straight line with each other. Now test the movement of the paddles with a fan (even the fan from an air conditioner compressor works for this) or with the wind, if there is more than a slight breeze. If the paddles are perfectly balanced they will remain in a horizontal position when resting.

Painting. Paint the penguin using this list of paints. Measurements are approximate. Paint all white areas first.

Tummy: ½ tsp. white/drop of burnt umber

Back wings, base: ¾ tsp. black

Beak, legs: 1/8 tsp. turner's yellow/drop of red

Eye: Dot of white/place a dot of black inside white dot towards the beak when white paint has dried

When dry, spray each piece of trim with a protective coat of semi-gloss lacquer.

Assembling. To attach the penguin's paddles, first check to see if any hot glue remains in the arm holes; if so, redrill the hole very carefully and the drill bit will pull out the dried glue. Mix epoxy and put some of this in the axle hole of the paddle. Insert the axle through the shoulders and put epoxy on each end of the axle. Do not use too much or you may end up with a paddle glued to your penguin. Press the first paddle on, then lay the penguin on his back. Push the other paddle on so that one paddle is up and the other down. Rest something under the paddles, if necessary, to keep them lined up straight. Let them dry completely.

Cut the $\frac{3}{16}$-in. metal rod with cutters to the desired length, depending on whether you use a base or not. Sand one end to a dull point with emery cloth. Insert this end into the penguin and then place him on the base or outdoors to whirl his wings in the wind.

Rabbit

MATERIALS

Pine, ¾ in. thick: 6 × 12 in.
Metal rod, ⅛ in. diameter: 2 in. long
Metal rod, 3⁄16 in. diameter: 2½ in. long if it is to be mounted on a base or 15 to 36 in. long if not
Acrylic paint: titanium white, burnt umber, naphthol red light, turner's yellow
Sandpaper: medium and fine grades
Emery cloth
Tracing paper
Poster board
Semi-gloss lacquer spray

TOOLS

Scroll saw or band saw
Drill with ⅛, 9⁄64, 3⁄16, and 7⁄32-in. bits

Illus. 38.

Stationary belt sander or sanding wheel: with medium-grade sandpaper
Metal cutters
Hot glue gun (optional): for testing paddles on dummy

INSTRUCTIONS

Pattern. Trace all the pattern pieces and transfer them onto poster board, including all paint lines. Cut out templates, cutting outline only. Trace pattern of rabbit and two carrot paddles onto the ¾-in. pine.

Cutting. Cut out all three pattern pieces, including a 3 × 3-in. square for the base.

Drilling. Drill a hole into each shoulder of paddle where marked with the ⅛-in. bit. All holes must be perfectly straight and centered. If possible, use a drill press. Drill a 9⁄64-in. hole through the rabbit's shoulder as indicated. Next drill a 7⁄32-in. hole up through the bottom of the rabbit and a 3⁄16-in. hole in the center of the base.

Cut off the top ⅜ in. of a flathead nail or tack with metal cutters. Insert this, flat side out, into the underside of the rabbit. Tap this in with a dowel, using a hammer if necessary (Illus. 13, p. 17).

Shaping Paddles. To form the rabbit's paddles first draw an angle line with a pencil from the top right corner to the bottom left corner on the end of each paddle. Hold the paddles side by side and make sure the paddles and angle lines are identical. It should appear that you are making two right arms/paddles; however—when placed on the other side—the arm will be reversed as it should be.

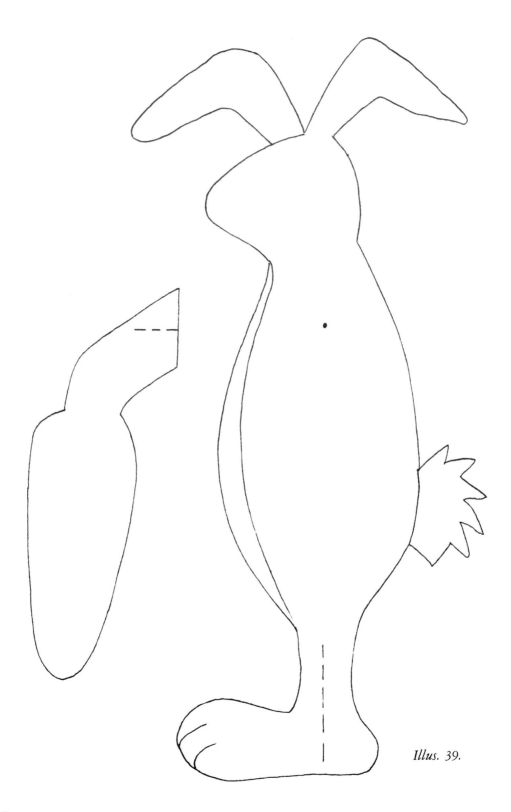

Illus. 39.

Pirate.

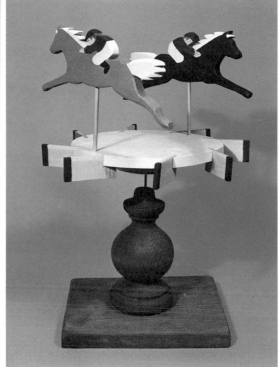

Racing jockeys.

Man milking cow.

A

Wizard.

Angel.

Fisherman.

Mermaid.

Sailor.

Uncle Sam.

Unicorn.

Rabbit.

Penguin.

D

Always paying attention to the drawn pencil angle, take the paddle in your hand and gently press it against the sander. Keep the pencil line *parallel* to the sander at all times. Move the paddle back and forth against the sander. After you have sanded a portion away on one side, turn the paddle over and start sanding on the other side. Keep sanding both sides until you reduce the paddle (not the shoulders) to approximately ⅛ in. to 3/16 in. (Illus. 17). It is very important to keep checking the angle. This is why I prefer the sanding wheel, as I can see the angle more easily. Repeat this procedure with the other paddle, making them as identical as possible.

Sanding. Using the sander, round the shoulder and arm of the paddles as much as possible. Also round the body edges, holding the edges at an angle to the sander to achieve a carved appearance. Sand the base piece. Give each piece a final sanding by hand with fine sandpaper.

Testing. Making a "dummy" whirligig out of ¾-in. scraps of wood, approximately 3 × 3 in. for a base and about 2½ × 10 in. for the body. Drill a 9/64-in. hole, about an inch from the top of the dummy body, through the center of the width and also through the center of the thickness. This way it can be used for any of the whirligigs. Cut the ⅛-in. rod to 2 in.

Apply a drop of hot glue on the drilled hole, then push the ⅛-in. rod into the hole. Put the axle through the dummy and then put another drop of glue on the

other paddle. Push the paddle onto the axle, with one paddle up and one paddle down so that the shoulders form a straight line with each other. Now test the movement of the paddles with a fan (even the fan from an air conditioner compressor works for this) or with the wind if there is more than a slight breeze. If the paddles are perfectly balanced they will remain in a horizontal position when resting.

Painting. Mix paints as given below. Paint tummy area first. All proportions are approximate.
Tummy, tail: ¼ tsp. white/drop of burnt umber
Carrots: ⅛ tsp. red/⅛ tsp. yellow
Rabbit body: ¼ tsp. white/¼ tsp. burnt umber
Base: ¼ tsp. red/¼ tsp. burnt umber
Paint a dot of white for the eye. Let it dry and then paint a dot of black on the white, towards the nose.

When dry, spray with a protective semi-gloss lacquer.

Assembling. To attach the paddles first check to see if any hot glue remains in the arm holes; if so, redrill the hole very carefully and the drill bit will pull out the dried glue. Mix epoxy and put some of this in the axle hole of the paddle. Insert the axle through the shoulders and put epoxy on each end of the axle. Do not use too much or you may end up with a paddle glued to your rabbit. Press the first paddle on, then lay the rabbit on his back. Push the other paddle on so that one paddle is up and the other is down.

Rest something under the paddles, if necessary to keep them lined up straight. Let them dry completely.

Cut the ⅜₆-in. metal rod with cutters, to desired length, and sand one end to a dull point with emery cloth. Insert this end of the rod into the rabbit. If you are using a base, push the other end of the rod into it.

If your rabbit is going outdoors, put him on the rod and attach him to a fence post, mailbox or wherever there is a breeze.

Santa

MATERIALS

Pine, ¾ in. thick: 12 × 18 in.
Metal rod, ⅛ in. diameter: 2½ in. long
Metal rod, 3⁄16 in. diameter: 4 in. long if it
is to be mounted on a base or 15 to 36
in. long if not
Acrylic paint: naphthol red light, mars
black, titanium white, burnt umber, per-
manent green deep
Brushes: ½ in. and ¼ in.
Sandpaper: medium and fine grades

Emery cloth
Epoxy glue
Tracing paper
Poster board
Semi-gloss lacquer spray
Permanent, black, fine-tip marker

TOOLS

Scroll saw or band saw
Drill with ⅛, 9⁄64, 3⁄16, and 7⁄32-in. bits
Stationary belt sander or sanding wheel:
with medium-grade sandpaper
Metal cutters
Hot glue gun (optional): for testing pad-
dles on dummy

INSTRUCTIONS

Pattern. Trace all the pattern pieces for
Santa and transfer them onto poster
board, including all paint lines. Cut out
templates, cutting outline only. Trace pattern pieces onto the pine board.

Cutting. Cut the pieces for Santa, plus
two base pieces, 3¼ × 6 in. and 4¼ ×
7½ in. out of the ¾-in. wood.

Drilling. Drill a ⅛-in.-diameter hole into
each shoulder piece of the Santa as
marked. Be sure to drill as straight and
even as possible, using a drill press if
available. Drill a hole for the axle
through the body of Santa as indicated,
with the 9⁄64-in. drill bit. Next, drill a 7⁄32-
in. hole into the bottom of Santa for the
pivot rod. Use the 3⁄16-in. bit to drill a
hole through the center of the 3¼ × 6-
in. base piece.

Cut off the top ⅜ in. of a flathead tack or
nail with metal cutters and insert this, flat
side out, into the hole in the underside of

Illus. 40.

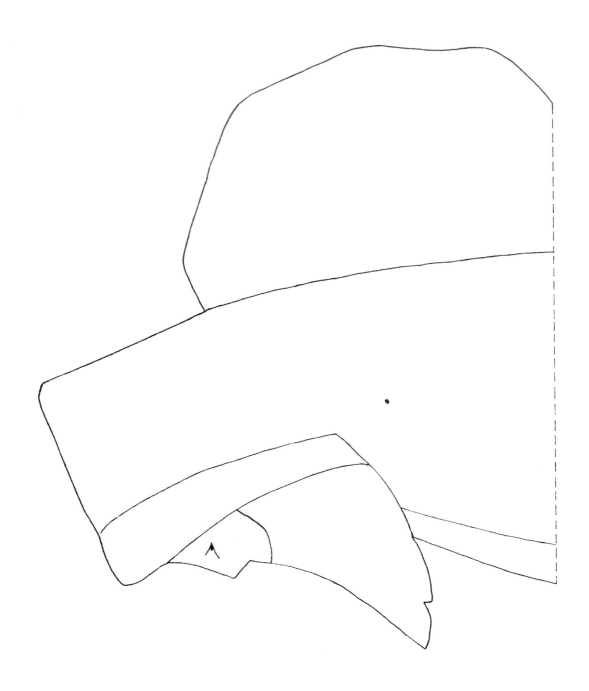

Illus. 41.

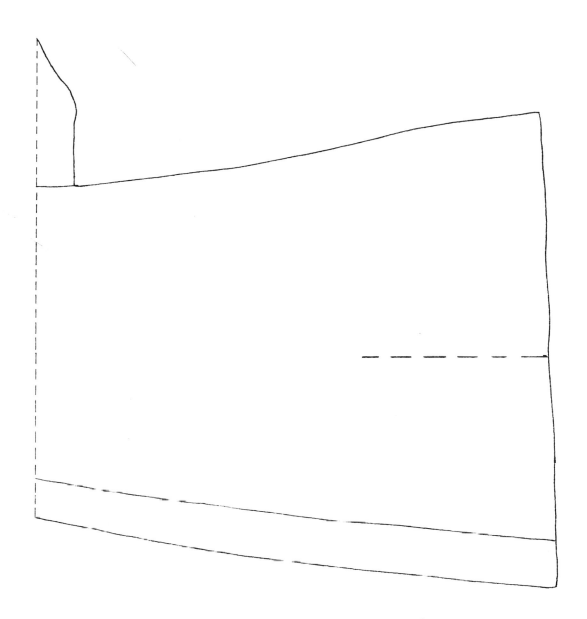

Paddle pattern on next page

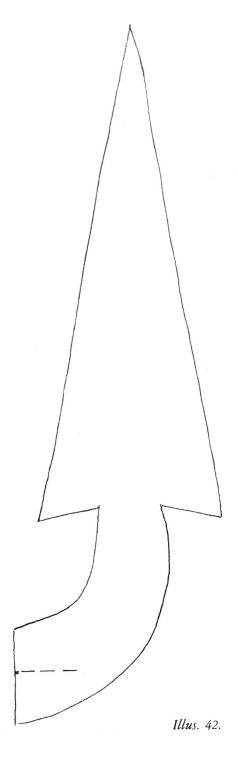

Illus. 42.

Santa. This gives the pivot rod a smooth spinning surface (Illus. 13, p. 17).

Shaping Paddles. To form Santa's paddles, draw an angle line with a pencil from the top right side of the paddle point, cross through the center of the point, to the left side of the point. Make sure the paddles and angle lines are identical. It should appear that you are making two right arms/paddles, however when placed on the other side the arm will be reversed as it should be.

Always paying attention to the drawn pencil angle, take the paddle in your hand and gently press it against the sander. Keep the pencil line *parallel* to the sander at all times. Move the paddle back and forth against the sander. After you have sanded a portion away on one side, turn the paddle over and start sanding on the other side. Keep sanding both sides until you reduce the paddle (not the shoulder) to approximately ⅛ to ³⁄₁₆ in. (Illus. 17). It is very important to keep checking the angle. This is why I prefer the sanding wheel, as I can see the angle more easily. Repeat this procedure with the other paddle, making them as identical as possible.

Sanding. Round the shoulder and arm of the paddles as much as possible with the sander. Also round the body edges, holding the edges at an angle to the sander to achieve a carved appearance. Sand all base pieces. Give each piece a final sanding by hand with fine sandpaper.

Testing. Make a "dummy" whirligig out of ¾-in. scraps of wood, approximately 3

X 3 in. for a base and about 2½ X 10 in. for the body. Drill a ⁹⁄₆₄-in. hole, about an inch from the top of the dummy body, through the center of the width and also through the center of the thickness. This way it can be used for any of the whirligigs. Cut the ⅛-in. rod to 2½ in.

Apply a drop of hot glue on the drilled hole, then push the ⅛-in. rod into the hole. Put the axle through the dummy and then put another drop of glue on the other paddle. Push the paddle onto the axle, with one paddle up, one paddle down so that the shoulders form a straight line with each other. Now test the movement of the paddles with a fan (even the fan from an air conditioner compressor works for this) or with the wind, if there is more than a slight breeze. If the paddles are perfectly balanced they will remain in a horizontal position when resting.

Painting. When you are satisfied with the paddles, then you can proceed with painting Santa. Follow the approximate proportions of paint below, starting with the white areas.
Beard, trim: ¾ tsp. white/drop of burnt umber
Bag: ¼ tsp. burnt umber/¼ tsp. white
Trees: ½ tsp. green/drop of black
Coat: 1½ tsp. red/few drops of black
Base: 1½ tsp. green/drop of black
To color the cheeks twist a paper napkin

into a point, dip only the very tip into red paint and then rub in a small circular motion. Try this on scrap wood first to practice getting the effect you want. Paint the eyes black or use a permanent black marker.

When dry, spray with a protective coating of semi-gloss lacquer.

Assembling. To attach the paddles, first check to see if any hot glue remains in the arm holes; if so, redrill the hole very carefully and the drill bit will pull out the dried glue. Mix epoxy and put some of this in the axle hole of the paddle. Insert the axle through the shoulders and put epoxy on each end of the axle. Do not use too much or you may end up with a paddle glued to Santa. Press the first paddle on, then lay Santa on his back. Push the other paddle on so that one paddle is up and the other down. Rest something under the paddles, if necessary, to keep them lined up straight. Let them dry completely.

Glue the small base piece on top of the large base piece. Cut the ³⁄₁₆-in. metal rod with cutter to the length desired and sand one end to a dull point with emery cloth. Place Santa on the rod and then set it into the base or, if your Santa will be blowing in the wind, place him on the longer rod and set him up outside.

Angel

MATERIALS

Pine, ¾ in. thick: 8 × 13 in.
Pine, ¾ in. thick (for optional base): 5½
× 5½ in.
Wooden dowel, ³⁄₁₆ in. diameter: 2 in.
long
Turned chair leg (for optional base): 6 in.
long
Metal rod, ⅛ in. diameter: 2¾ in. long
Metal rod, ³⁄₁₆ in. diameter: 3 in. long if it
is to be mounted on a base or 15 to 36
in. long if not
Acrylic paint: titanium white, turner's yellow, permanent green deep, naphthol red
light, mars black
Stain: medium color

Illus. 43.

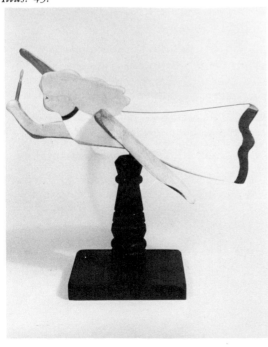

Semi-gloss lacquer spray
Brushes: ½ in., ¼ in.
Sandpaper: medium and fine grades
Emery cloth
Epoxy glue
Wood glue
Tracing paper
Poster board
Permanent, black, fine-point marker

TOOLS

Scroll saw or band saw
Drill with ⅛, ⁹⁄₆₄, ³⁄₁₆, and ⁷⁄₃₂-in. bits
Stationary belt sander or sanding wheel:
with medium-grade sandpaper
Metal cutters
Hot glue gun (optional): for testing pad-
dles on dummy

INSTRUCTIONS

Pattern. Trace both pattern pieces and
transfer onto poster board, including the
paint lines. Cut out templates, cutting
around outline only. Trace these patterns
onto the ¾-in. wood, making sure to
trace two paddles.

Cutting. Cut out the pieces for the angel
and then cut a 5½ × 5½-in. base piece
also from ¾-in. wood. Cut a 2-in. length
of ³⁄₁₆-in. dowel for the candle.

Drilling. Drill a ⅛-in.-diameter hole into
the shoulder area of both paddles, as
marked. Be sure all holes are drilled as
straight as possible. Use a drill press if
available. Drill a hole for the axle
through the body of the angel with the
⁹⁄₆₄-in. bit. Drill a hole in the underside of
the angel at the angle indicated on the
pattern with the ⁷⁄₃₂-in. bit. Drill a ³⁄₁₆-in.

hole in the angel's hand to hold the candle and then, using this same bit, drill a hole into the inverted chair leg (optional base piece). Cut off the top ⅜ in. flat head of a tack or nail with metal cutters and insert this, flat side out, into the hole on the underside of the angel. Tap it in with a dowel, using a hammer if necessary (Illus. 13, p. 17).

Shaping Paddles. To retain the basic shape of the paddle wing, be sure not to sand at an angle greater than the angle line drawn from side to side.

To form the paddles of the angel, first draw an angled line on the tip of the paddle (approximately 45° where the line meets the flat side). Since the paddle is curved at the end, this is done by first drawing a line at the tip of the paddle, from top to bottom and then marking the center of the line. Then draw equal lines on both sides of this line when drawing the 45° angle (Illus. 34, p. 35). Lay the paddles side by side and make sure the paddles and angle lines are identical. It should appear that you are making two right wing paddles; however, when placed on the other side the wing will be reversed as it should be.

Always paying attention to the drawn pencil angle, take the paddle in your hand and gently press it against the sander. Keep the pencil line *parallel* to the sander at all times. Move the paddle back and forth against the sander. After you have sanded a portion away on one side, turn the paddle over and start sanding on the other side. Keep sanding both sides until

you reduce the paddle (not the shoulder) to approximately ⅛ to 3/16 in. (Illus. 17). It is very important to keep checking the angle. This is why I prefer the sanding wheel, as I can see the angle more easily. Repeat this procedure with the other paddle, making them as identical as possible. Cut out a small curved section as shown on the pattern to finish the wing.

Sanding. Round the shoulder area of the paddles as much as possible with the sander. Keep the side of the paddle that will be against the body as flat as possible. Do not round these edges. Round the body edges, holding the edges at an angle to the sander to achieve a carved appearance. Sand the base piece. Give each piece a final sanding by hand with fine sandpaper and sand a groove to define the flame of the candle. Then sand a point on the end of the candle.

Testing. Make a "dummy" whirligig out of ¾-in. scraps of wood, approximately 3 × 3 in. for a base and about 2½ × 10 in. for the body. Drill a 9/64-in. hole about an inch from the top of the dummy body, through the center of the width and also through the center of the thickness. This way it can be used for any of the whirligigs. Cut the ⅛-in. rod to 2¾ in.

Apply a drop of hot glue on the drilled hole, then push the ⅛-in. rod into the hole. Put the axle through the dummy and then put another drop of glue on the other paddle. Push the paddle onto the axle with one paddle up, one paddle down so that the shoulders form a straight line with each other. Now test

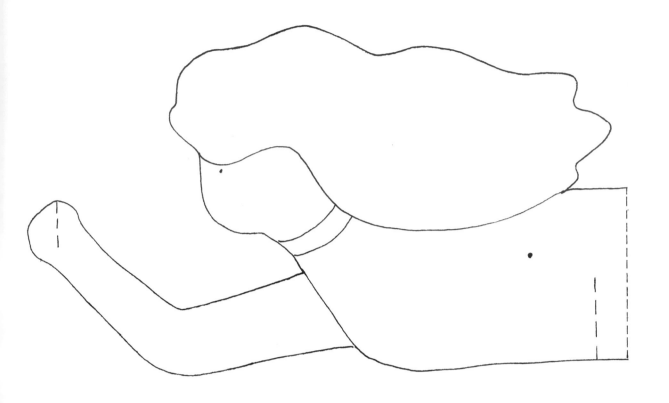

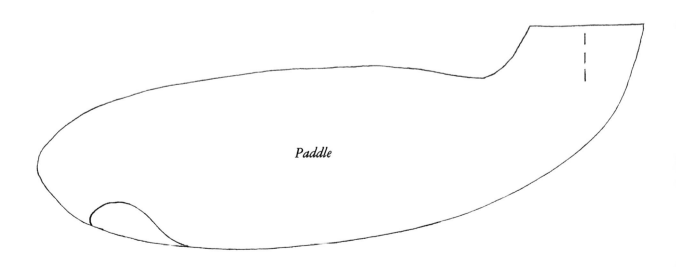

Paddle

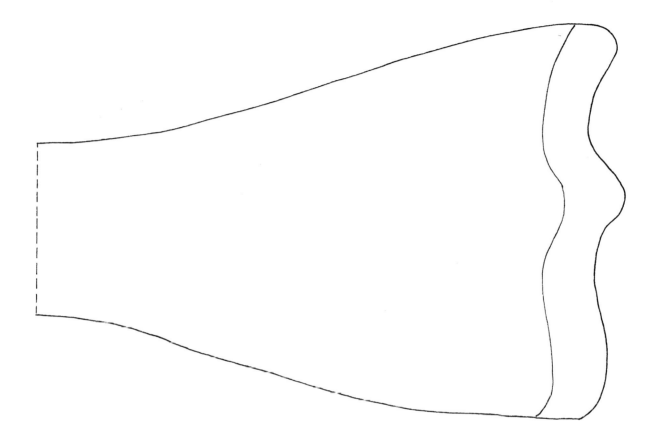

Illus. 44.

the movement of the paddles with a fan (even the fan from an air conditioner compressor works for this) or with the wind, if there is more than a slight breeze. If the paddles are perfectly balanced they will remain in a horizontal position when resting.

Painting. Using the approximate proportions listed, paint the angel. Start with white first.
Dress: 1 tsp. white
Hair: ½ tsp. yellow
Trim: ½ tsp. green
Base: 1 tsp. green
Candle base: drop of red
Flame: drop of red/drop of yellow

Staining. Rub a light coat of medium-color stain over the angel and her wings with a small cloth. Wipe off any excess immediately. Spray with a protective coating of semi-gloss lacquer when dry.

Assembling. Glue the base pieces together if you are using a base. To attach the paddles of the angel, first check to see if any hot glue remains in the arm holes;

if so, redrill the holes of the paddle very carefully and the drill bit will pull out the dried glue. Mix epoxy and put some of this in the axle hole of the paddles. A toothpick is handy for this.

Insert the axle through the shoulder and put a small amount of epoxy on each end of the axle. Do not use too much or you may end up with a paddle glued to the angel. Press the first paddle on, then prop the angel in her flying position. Push the other paddle on so that one paddle is forward and the other is back.

Set a scrap of wood under the paddles while drying in order to keep the shoulders in a straight line. Let them dry completely.

Cut the $\frac{3}{16}$-in. metal rod with cutters to desired length and sand one end to a dull point with emery cloth. Insert the pointed end into the underside of the angel. Either insert the other end into the base, if you are using your whirligig as folk art indoors, or put her outside to fly in the wind.

Watermelon Man

MATERIALS

Pine, ¾ in. thick: 8 × 12 in.
Metal rod, ⅛ in. diameter: 3¼ in. long
Metal rod, ³⁄₁₆ in. diameter: 4 in. long if it
is to be mounted on a base or 15 to 20
in. long if not

Illus. 45.

Acrylic paint: titanium white, mars black,
naphthol red light, permanent green deep
Stain: medium color
Brush: ¼ in., small round ¹⁄₁₆ in.
Sandpaper: medium and fine grades
Emery cloth
Epoxy glue
Tracing paper
Poster board
Semi-gloss lacquer spray
Permanent, black, fine-tip marker

TOOLS

Scroll saw or band saw
Drill with ⅛, ⁹⁄₆₄, ³⁄₁₆ and ⁷⁄₃₂-in. bits
Stationary belt sander or sanding wheel:
with medium-grade sandpaper
Metal cutters
Hot glue gun (optional): for testing pad-
dles on dummy

INSTRUCTIONS

Pattern. Trace the pattern pieces for the
watermelon man and his paddles. Transfer
them onto the poster board and cut out
around the outline. Trace all pattern
pieces onto the wood.

Cutting. Cut out all the pieces, including
a 3 × 3-in. square for the base, with the
scroll or band saw.

Drilling. Drill a ⅛-in.-diameter hole into
the center of each shoulder area of the
paddle. Next, drill a ⁹⁄₆₄-in.-diameter hole
through the shoulder area of the man. For
perfectly straight holes use a drill press, if
you have access to one. Now, drill a ⁷⁄₃₂-
in.-diameter hole through the legs of the
man and then drill one more hole, a ³⁄₁₆
in., in the center of the base. Cut off the

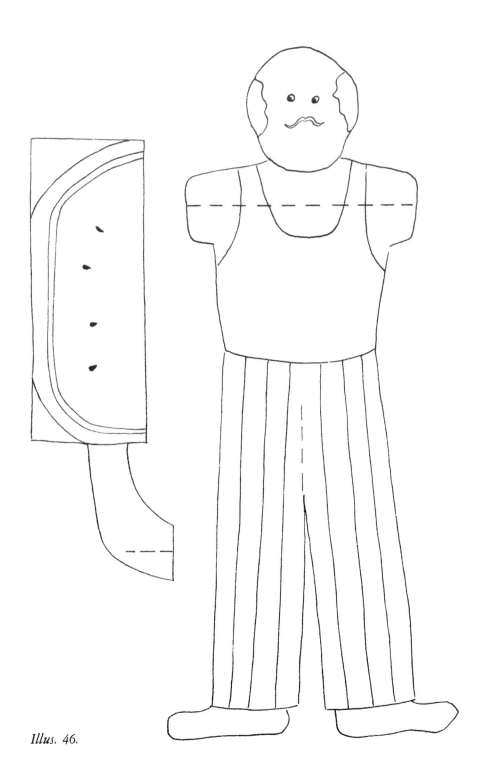

Illus. 46.

top ⅜ in. of a flathead nail or tack with metal cutters. Insert this, flat side out, into the hole between the legs. Tap it in with a dowel; if necessary use a hammer (Illus. 13, p. 17).

Shaping Paddles. To form the man's paddles, first draw an angle line with a pencil from the top right corner to the bottom left corner on the end of each paddle. Hold the paddles side by side and make sure the paddles and angle lines are identical. It should appear that you are making two right arms/paddles; however, when placed on the other side the arm will be reversed as it should be.

Always paying attention to the drawn pencil angle, take the paddle in your hand and gently press it against the sander. Keep the pencil line *parallel* to the sander at all times (Illus. 47). Move the paddle back and forth against the sander. After you have sanded a portion away on one side, turn the paddle over and start sanding on the other side. Keep sanding both sides until you reduce the paddle (not the shoulder) to approximately ⅛ to ³⁄₁₆ in. It is very important to keep checking the angle. This is why I prefer the sanding wheel, as I can see the angle more easily. Repeat this procedure with the other paddle, making them as identical as possible.

Illus. 47.

Carefully cut off a rounded corner to form a watermelon from each paddle.

Sanding. Round the shoulder and arm of the paddles as much as possible with the sander. Keep the side of the paddle that will be against the body as flat as possible. Do not round these edges. Round the body edges, holding the edges at an angle to the sander to achieve a carved appearance. Sand the base piece. Give each piece a final sanding by hand with fine sandpaper.

Testing. Make a "dummy" whirligig out of ¾-in. scraps of wood, approximately 3 × 3-in. for a base and about 2½ × 10-in. for the body. Drill a ⁹⁄₆₄-in. hole about an inch from the top of the dummy body through the center of the width and also through the center of the thickness. This way it can be used for any of the whirligigs. Cut the ⅛-in. rod to 3¼ in.

Painting. Paint the watermelon man using the approximate proportions given. Always paint lightest areas first, ending with the darkest.
Shirt, base: 1 tsp. white
Stripes, watermelon: 1 tsp. red/drop of black
Stripes, hair: ½ tsp. black
Watermelon rind: ¼ tsp. green/drop of black (leave a space of natural wood between red and green areas)
Paint a small dot of white for the eye.

When it is dry paint a small black dot inside the white dot.

Staining. Stain arms and man (do not stain the watermelons) with a cloth. Wipe off excess. When the stain is completely dry, spray the man with a protective coat of semi-gloss lacquer. Draw the moustache and the seeds of the watermelons with a black, permanent, fine-tip marker.

Assembling. To attach the watermelon paddles, first check to see if any hot glue remains in the arm holes; if so, redrill the hole very carefully and the drill bit will pull out the dried glue. Mix the epoxy and put some of it in the axle hole of the paddle. Insert the axle through the shoulders and put epoxy on each end of the axle. Do not use too much or you may end up with a paddle glued to your watermelon man. Press the first paddle on, then lay him on his back. Push the other paddle on so that one paddle is up and the other down. Rest something under the paddles, if necessary, to keep them lined up straight. Let them dry completely.

Cut the ³⁄₁₆-in. metal rod with cutters to the desired length, depending on whether you use a base or not. Sand one end to a dull point with emery cloth. Insert this end into the watermelon man and then place him on the base or outside and watch him whirl!

Wizard

MATERIALS

Pine, ¾ in. thick: 7 × 10 in.

Pine, ¾ in. thick: (2-tier base, optional): 7 × 11 in.

Metal rod, ⅛ in. diameter: 3⅞ in. long

Metal rod, ³⁄₁₆ in. diameter: 3½ in. long if it is to be mounted on a base or 15 to 20 in. long if not

Acrylic paint: deep brilliant red, cerulean blue hue, titanium white, burnt umber

Brushes: ½ in. and ¼ in.

Semi-gloss lacquer spray

Sandpaper: medium and fine grades

Emery cloth

Wood glue

Epoxy glue

Tracing paper

Poster board

Permanent, black, fine-tip marker

TOOLS

Scroll saw or band saw

Drill with ⅛, ⁹⁄₆₄, ³⁄₁₆, and ⁷⁄₃₂-in. bits

Stationary belt sander or sanding wheel: with medium-grade sandpaper

Metal cutters

Hot glue gun (optional): for testing paddles on dummy

INSTRUCTIONS

Pattern. Trace the pattern pieces for the wizard and transfer them onto the poster board, including the paint lines. Cut out templates, cutting around the outline only. Trace these patterns onto the ¾-in. wood, making sure to trace two paddles.

Cutting. Cut out the three pieces for the wizard and then cut out two circles, one 4½ in. in diameter, the other 6 in. in diameter. These are the optional base pieces.

Drilling. Drill a ⅛-in.-diameter hole into the shoulder area of each paddle, as marked. Drill as straight as possible. Use a drill press if you have access to one. All holes must be straight to ensure proper movement of your whirligig. Drill a hole for the axle through the shoulder area of the body piece with the ⁹⁄₆₄-in. drill bit. Next, drill a ⁷⁄₃₂-in.-diameter hole into the bottom of the wizard, as indicated on the pattern. Use the ³⁄₁₆-in. bit to drill a hole into the center of the smallest circle base.

Illus. 48.

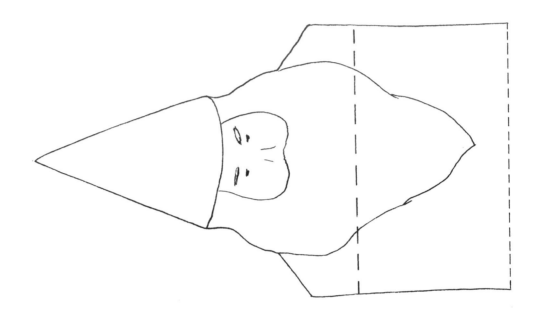

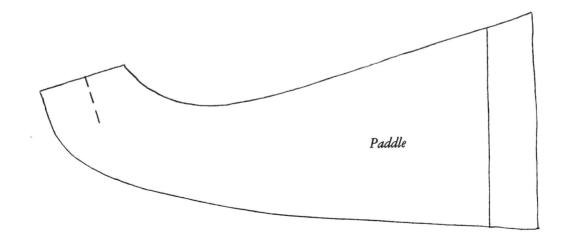

Paddle

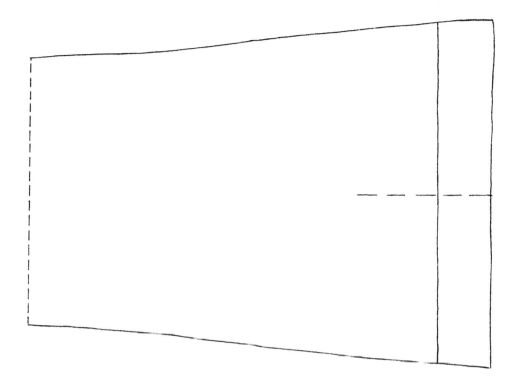

Illus. 49.

Cut off the top ⅜ in. of a flathead tack or nail with metal cutters and insert this, flat side out, into the hole in the underside of the wizard. Tap it in with a dowel, using a hammer if necessary. This will give the rod a smooth spinning surface (Illus. 13, p. 17).

Shaping Paddles. To form the wizard's paddles, first draw an angle line with a pencil from the top right corner to the bottom left corner on the end of each paddle. Hold the paddles side by side and make sure the paddles and angle lines are identical. It should appear that you are making two right arms/paddles; however, when placed on the other side the arm will be reversed as it should be.

Always paying attention to the drawn pencil angle, take the paddle in your hand and gently press it against the sander. Keep the pencil line *parallel* to the sander at all times. Move the paddle back and forth against the sander. After you have sanded a portion away on one side, turn the paddle over and start sanding on the other side. Keep sanding both sides until you reduce the paddle (not the shoulder) to approximately ⅛ to ³⁄₁₆ in. (Illus. 17). It is very important to keep checking the angle. This is why I prefer the sanding wheel, as I can see the angle more easily. Repeat this procedure with the other paddle, making them as identical as possible.

Sanding. Round the shoulder and arm of the paddles as much as possible with the sander. Keep the side of the paddle that will be against the body as flat as possible. Do not round these edges. Round the

body edges, holding the edges at an angle to the sander to achieve a carved appearance. Sand all base pieces. Give each piece a final sanding by hand with fine sandpaper.

Testing. Make a "dummy" whirligig out of ¾-in. scraps of wood, approximately 3 × 3-in. for a base and about 2½ × 10-in. for the body. Drill a ⁹⁄₆₄-in. hole about an inch from the top of the dummy body, through the center of the width and through the center of the thickness. This way, it can be used for any of the whirligigs. Cut the ⅛-in. rod to 3⅞ in.

Apply a drop of hot glue on the drilled hole, then push the ⅛-in. rod into the hole. Put the axle through the dummy and then put another drop of glue on the other paddle. Push the paddle onto the axle, with one paddle up and one paddle down so that the shoulders form a straight line with each other. Now test the movement of the paddles with a fan (even the fan from an air conditioner compressor works for this) or with the wind, if there is more than a slight breeze. If the paddles are perfectly balanced they will remain in a horizontal position when resting.

Painting. When you are satisfied with the paddles you can proceed with the painting. Use the approximate proportions of paint below, starting with the white areas. Refer to your pattern for paint lines.
Beard, trim, eyebrows: ¼ tsp. white/drop of burnt umber
Robe, hat: ½ tsp. red/½ tsp. blue

Bases: water down ½ tsp. red/½ tsp. blue and paint with this "wash"

When dry, spray all pieces with a protective coat of semi-gloss lacquer. Then draw eyes with a permanent, black, fine-tip marker.

Assembling. To attach the paddles of the wizard, first check to see if any hot glue remains in the arm holes; if so, redrill the hole very carefully and the drill bit will pull out the dried glue. Mix the epoxy and put some of it in the axle hole of the paddle. Insert the axle through the shoulders and put epoxy on each end of the axle. Do not use too much or you may end up with a paddle glued to the wizard. Press the first paddle on, then lay the wizard on his back. Push the other paddle on so that one paddle is up and the other down. Rest something under the paddles, if necessary, to keep them lined up straight. Let them dry competely.

Glue the small base piece on top of the large base piece. Cut the $3/16$-in. metal rod with a cutter to the length desired and sand one end to a dull point with emery cloth. Place the wizard on the rod and then set into the base or, if your wizard will be blowing in the wind, place him on the longer rod and set him up outside.

Unicorn

MATERIALS

Pine, ¾ in. thick: 8 × 11 in.
Wooden dowel, ⁄₁₆ in. diameter: 1¾ in. long for horn
Metal rod, ⅛ in. diameter: 2¼ in. long
Metal rod, ⁄₁₆ in. diameter: 3¼ in. long if it is to be mounted on a base or 10 to 15 in. long if not
Acrylic paint: titanium white, burnt umber, turner's yellow, mars black
Semi-gloss lacquer spray
Sandpaper: medium and fine grades
Emery cloth
Epoxy glue
Tracing paper
Poster board

TOOLS

Scroll saw or band saw
Drill with ⅛, ⁹⁄₆₄, ⁷⁄₃₂, and ⁄₁₆-in. bits
Stationary belt sander or sanding wheel: with medium-grade sandpaper
Metal cutters
Hot glue gun (optional): for testing paddles on dummy

INSTRUCTIONS

Pattern. Trace both pattern pieces for the unicorn and transfer them onto poster

Illus. 50.

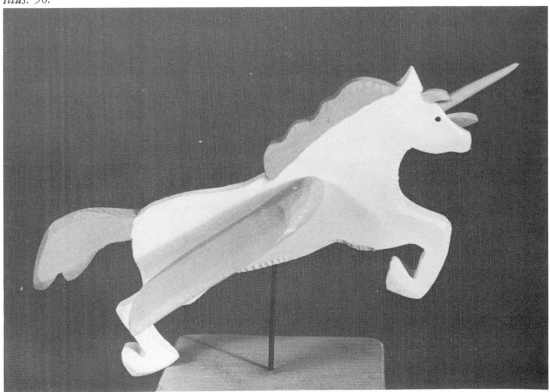

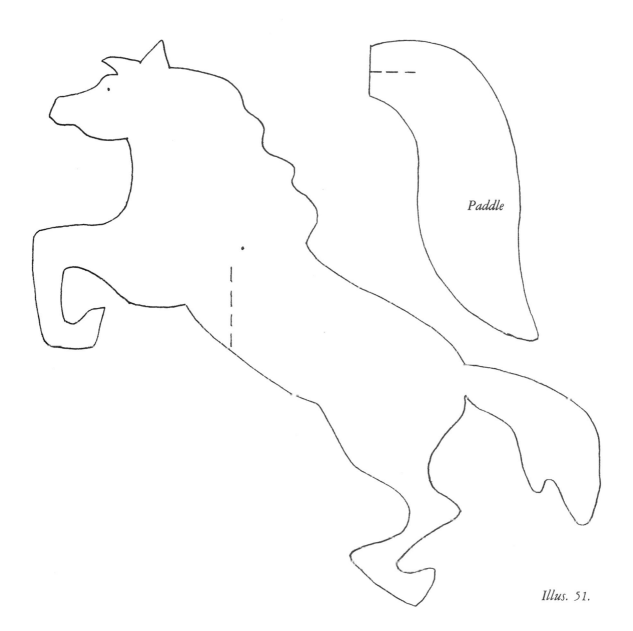

Paddle

Illus. 51.

board. Cut out templates, cutting around the outline only. Trace pattern pieces for one unicorn and two wings onto the ¾-in. wood.

Cutting. Cut out all three pieces for the whirligig and then cut a 3⅜ × 3⅜-in. base piece from the same wood. Cut a 1¾-in. long dowel, ³⁄₁₆ in. diameter for the horn.

Drilling. Drill a ⅛ in.-diameter hole into the shoulder area of each paddle. Drill as straight as possible, using a drill press if available. Drill a hole through the shoulder area of the unicorn, as marked, with the ⁹⁄₆₄-in. bit. Next, drill a ⁷⁄₃₂-in.-diameter hole into the underside of the body at the angle marked on the pattern. Finally, drill a ³⁄₁₆-in.-diameter hole into the center of the base and also into the forehead of the unicorn, just beneath the forelock.

Cut off the top ⅜ in. of a flathead nail or tack with metal cutters and insert this, flat side out, into the hole on the underside of the unicorn. Tap this in with a dowel, using a hammer if necessary (Illus. 13, p. 17).

Shaping Paddles. To retain the basic shape of the paddle wing be sure not to sand at an angle greater than the angle line drawn from side to side.

To form the paddles of the unicorn, first draw an angled line on the tip of the paddle (approximately 45° where the line meets the flat side). Since the paddle is curved at the end first draw a line at the tip of the paddle, from top to bottom and then mark the center of the line. Then

draw equal lines on both sides of this line when drawing the 45° angle (Illus. 34, p. 35). Lay the paddles side by side and make sure the paddles and angle lines are identical. It should appear that you are making two right paddles; however, when placed on the other side the wing will be reversed as it should be.

Always paying attention to the drawn pencil angle, take the paddle in your hand and gently press it against the sander.

Keep the pencil line *parallel* to the sander at all times. Move the paddle back and forth against the sander. After you have sanded a portion away on one side, turn the paddle over and start sanding on the other side. Keep sanding both sides until you reduce the paddle (not the shoulder) to approximately ⅛ to ³⁄₁₆ in. (Illus. 17). It is very important to keep checking the angle. This is why I prefer the sanding wheel, as I can see the angle more easily. Repeat this procedure with the other paddle, making them as identical as possible.

Sanding. Round the shoulder and wings of the paddles as much as possible with the sander. Keep the side of the paddle that will be against the body as flat as possible. Do not round these edges. Round the body edges, holding the edges at an angle to the sander to achieve a carved appearance. Sand the horn to a gradual point. Give each piece a final sanding by hand with fine sandpaper.

Testing. Make a "dummy" whirligig out of ¾-in. scraps of wood, approximately 3 × 3-in. for a base and about 2½ × 10-in.

for the body. Drill a ⁹⁄₆₄-in. hole about an inch from the top of the dummy body, through the center of the width and through the center of the thickness. This way it can be used for any of the whirligigs. Cut the ⅛-in. rod to 2¼ in.

Apply a drop of hot glue on the drilled hole, then push the ⅛-in. rod into the hole. Put the axle through the dummy and then put another drop of glue on the other paddle. Push the paddle onto the axle with one paddle up, one paddle down, so that the shoulders form a straight line with each other. Now test the movement of the paddles with a fan (even the fan from an air conditioner compressor works for this) or with the wind, if there is more than a slight breeze. If the paddles are perfectly balanced they will remain in a horizontal position when resting.

Painting. Paint the unicorn using the approximate proportions listed.
Unicorn body: ½ tsp. white/drop of burnt umber
Tail, mane, wings: ½ tsp. white/¼ tsp. burnt umber
Horn: drop of yellow
Eye: paint a small dot of white/on top of this (after it dries) paint a smaller dot of black

Spray all of the pieces with a protective coating of the semi-gloss lacquer.

Assembling. To attach paddles of the unicorn, first check to see if any hot glue remains in the arm holes; if so, redrill the holes of the paddle very carefully and the drill bit will pull out the dried glue. Mix the epoxy and put some of this in the axle hole of the paddles. A toothpick is handy for this.

Insert the axle through the shoulder and put a small amount of epoxy on each end of the axle. Do not use too much or you may end up with a paddle glued to your unicorn. Press the first paddle on, then prop the unicorn up in his flying position. Push the other paddle on so that one paddle is forward and the other is back. Set a scrap of wood under the paddles while drying in order to keep the shoulders in a straight line. Let dry completely. Apply a drop of glue to the unicorn's horn and insert it into the pre-drilled hole. Let this dry.

Cut the ³⁄₁₆-in. metal rod with cutters to your desired length and sand one end to a dull point with emery cloth. Insert the pointed end into the underside of the unicorn. Either insert the other end into the base, if you are using your whirligig as folk art, or put him outside to whirl in the wind.

Whirligigs: Propeller Paddle

Grasshopper

MATERIALS

Pine, ¾ in. thick: 8 × 15 in.
Birch plywood, ¼ in. thick: 4 × 6 in.
4 × 4 lumber, 4 in. diameter: 6 in. long
for optional base
Metal rod, ³⁄₁₆ in. diameter: 6½ in. long if
it is to be mounted on a base or 15 to 36
in. long if not
Metal rod, ¹⁄₃₂ in. diameter: 6 in. long for
antennae
Flathead wood screws, 2½ in. × 6: two
Fender washers, ⅛ × ¾ in.: two
Wooden dowels, ⅝ in. diameter: two 1³⁄₁₆
in. lengths

Acrylic paint: titanium white, chromium
oxide green, naphthol red light, burnt
umber, mars black
Brush: ½ in.
Semi-gloss lacquer spray
Sandpaper: medium and fine grades
Emery cloth
Wood glue
Epoxy glue
Tracing paper
Poster board

TOOLS

Scroll saw or band saw
Coping saw (optional: see cutting directions)
Drill with ¹⁄₃₂, ³⁄₃₂, ⁵⁄₃₂, ⁷⁄₃₂, and ³⁄₁₆-in. bits

Illus. 52.

Stationary belt sander or sanding wheel: with medium- and fine-grade sandpaper
Metal cutters
Needle-nose pliers

INSTRUCTIONS

Pattern. Trace all the pattern pieces and transfer them onto poster board. Cut out templates, cutting around the outline only. Trace the pattern pieces for the body, two legs and two rectangles onto the ¾-in. pine. Trace four wings onto the ¼-in. birch.

Cutting. Cut out all pieces for the grasshopper whirligig with the scroll or band saw. Now draw a diagonal line from the left bottom corner to the right top corner on the 1⅛ × ¾-in. surface of the rectangular blocks. Draw identical lines on the opposite surface of the blocks. These are identical lines when viewing the surface straight on, but because they are 90° apart, they are actually reversed (Illus. 53).

Since the angle of this line is approximately 55°, it is difficult to cut with the band saw (most tabletops only tilt to 45°). However, you can prop a small strip of wood underneath the block to increase the angle. The easiest method is to use a coping saw. Either way, cut a groove, ¼ in. deep and approximately 7/32 in. wide. (The ¼-in. plywood is actually slightly narrower than its given dimensions.) Then cut two 1 3/16-in. lengths of ⅜-in.-diameter dowel, if you have not already done so. These are used as spacers.

Drilling. Drill two 1/32-in.-diameter holes into the head of the grasshopper at the angle shown on the pattern. These are for the antennae and should be approximately ⅜ in. apart. Drill a hole through the center of the grasshopper body, where marked, with the 3/32 in. bit. Then drill a 5/32-in.-diameter hole into the center of both rectangular blocks, as indicated on the pattern. Use this bit to drill a hole into the center of each 1 3/16-in. spacer. Then, using the 7/32-in. bit, drill a hole into the underside of the grasshopper for the pivot rod. Finally, drill a 3/16-in.-diameter hole into the center of the base.

Cut off the top ⅜ in. of a flathead nail or tack with metal cutters and insert this, flat side out, into the hole on the underside of the grasshopper. Tap this in with a

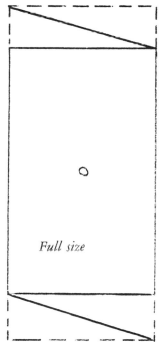

Illus. 53. Diagonal groove lines for rectangular blocks

Full size

Illus. 54.

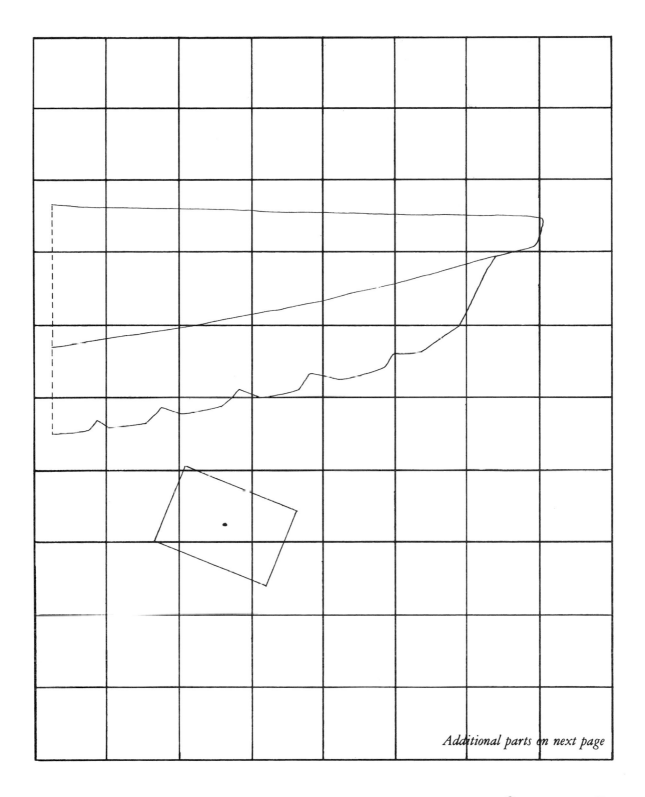

Additional parts on next page

Illus. 55.

dowel, using a hammer if necessary (Illus. 13, p. 17).

Sanding. Round edges as much as possible with the sander. This gives a nice carved appearance. It is not necessary to round the blocks or spacers. Sand all pieces by hand with fine-grade sandpaper. Sand square ends of wings to fit snugly into grooves. Then apply a thin layer of wood glue and push into grooves. Let it dry.

Painting. Paint the grasshopper using the approximate proportions given.
Belly, wings, spacers: 1½ tsp. green/ ¼ tsp. white
Grasshopper back: ½ tsp. green
Head, legs: ½ tsp. red/ ¼ tsp. burnt umber
Eye: drop of black

After all pieces have dried, spray them with a protective coating of semi-gloss lacquer.

Assembling. Attach the legs to the grasshopper with wood glue. Refer to the photo for placement. When this is dry, insert one of the flathead screws through the pre-drilled hole of the wing section, through a washer, and then through a spacer (Illus. 58). Screw this into the hole on the side of the grasshopper. Before repeating this procedure with the other wing section note that if both wings are attached identically to one another they will whirl in the same direction. If one is reversed they will whirl in opposite directions.

After fastening the other wing, cut two 2¼-in. lengths of ⅟₃₂-in.-diameter metal rod. Curve one end into an oval with needle-nose pliers. Mix a drop of epoxy and apply this to the straight end of the antennae. Insert antennae into the pre-drilled holes and set aside to dry.

Cut the ³⁄₁₆-in.-diameter metal rod to the desired length and sand the top of the rod to a dull point with emery cloth. Set the grasshopper on this end and insert the other end into the base or attach the grasshopper outdoors to whirl in the wind.

Canadian Goose

MATERIALS

Pine, ¾ in. thick: 5 × 18 in.
Birch plywood, ¼ in. thick: 6 × 10 in.
Pine for the base (optional): ¾ in. thick,
3⅓ × 7½ in.; 1 × 1½ lumber, 3½ in.
long
Metal rod, 3⁄16 in. diameter: 5 in. long if to
be mounted on a base or 15 to 36 in.
long if not
Flathead wood screws; 2⅓ in. × 6: two
Fender washers, ⅛ × ¾ in.: two
Wooden dowels, ⅝ in. diameter: two 13⁄16
in. lengths

Acrylic paint: titanium white, burnt
umber, mars black, turner's yellow,
naphthol red light
Brush: ½ in.
Semi-gloss lacquer spray
Sandpaper: medium and fine grades
Emery cloth
Wood glue
Epoxy glue
Tracing paper
Poster board

TOOLS

Scroll saw or band saw
Coping saw (optional: see cutting sec-
tion)
Drill with 3⁄32, 5⁄32, 7⁄32, 3⁄16-in. bits

Illus. 56.

98

Stationary belt sander or sanding wheel: with medium- and fine-grade sandpaper
Metal cutters

INSTRUCTIONS

Pattern. Trace all the pattern pieces and transfer them onto poster board. Cut out templates, cutting around the outline only. Trace the pattern pieces for the body and two rectangles onto the ¾-in. pine. Trace four wings onto the ¼-in. birch.

Cutting. Cut out all the pieces for the goose whirligig with the scroll or band saw. Now draw a diagonal line from the left bottom corner to the right top corner on the 1⅛ × ¾-in. surface of the rectangular blocks. Draw identical lines on the opposite surface of the blocks. These are identical lines when viewing the surface straight on but, because they are 90° apart, they are actually reversed. Since the angle of this line is approximately 55°, it is difficult to cut with the band saw (most tabletops only tilt to 45°). However, you can prop a small strip of wood underneath the block to increase the angle. The easiest tool to use is a coping saw. Either way, cut a groove, ¼ in. deep and approximately 7⁄32 in. wide. (The ¼-in. plywood is actually slightly narrower than this dimension.) Then cut two 1³⁄₁₆-in. lengths of ⅝-in.-diameter dowel, if you have not already done so. These are used as spacers. Cut two base pieces; the dimensions are given above under "Materials."

Drilling. Drill a hole through the center of the goose body, where marked, with the 3⁄32-in. bit. Then drill a 7⁄32-in.-diameter hole into the center of both rectangular blocks, as indicated on the pattern. Use this bit to drill a hole into the center of each 1³⁄₁₆-in. spacer. Then drill a hole into the underside of the goose for the pivot rod with the 7⁄32-in. bit. Finally, drill a 3⁄16-in.-diameter hole into the center of the 3½-in. long base piece.

Cut off the top ⅜ in. of a flathead nail or tack with metal cutters and insert this, flat side up, into the hole on the underside of the goose. Tap this in with a dowel, using a hammer if necessary.

Sanding. Round edges as much as possible with the sander. This gives a nice carved appearance. It is not necessary to round the blocks or spacers. Sand all pieces by hand with fine-grade sandpaper.

Sand the square ends of the wings to fit snugly into the grooves. Then apply a thin layer of wood glue and push into grooves. Let it dry.

Painting. Paint the Canadian goose using the approximate proportions given. Paint white areas first and finish with black. Refer to the pattern for correct paint lines.
Belly, markings: 1 tsp. white/ drop of burnt umber
Legs, beak: ¼ tsp. yellow/ drop of red/ drop of burnt umber
Entire wing area: 1 tsp. white/ 1 tsp. black
Base pieces: 1 tsp. black

Illus. 57.

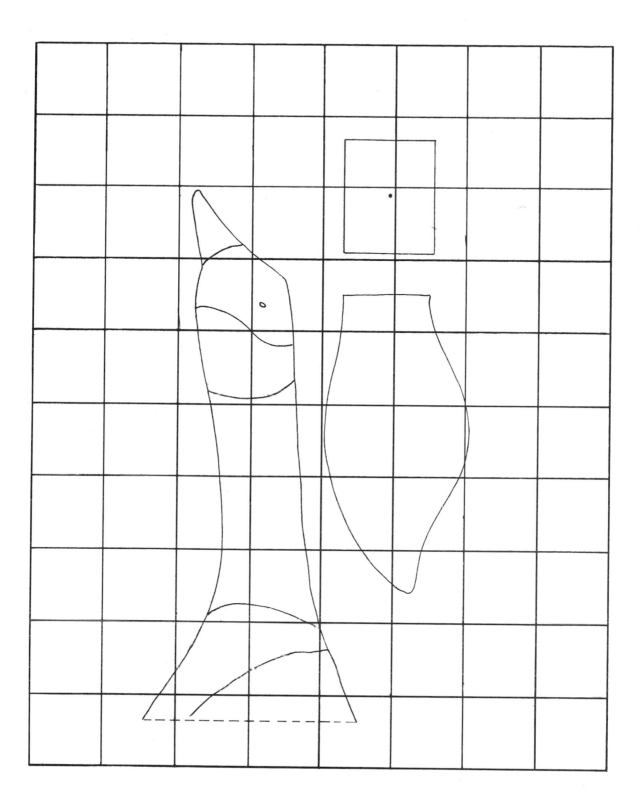

After all pieces have dried, spray them with a protective coating of semi-gloss lacquer.

Assembling. Insert one of the flathead screws through the pre-drilled hole of the wing section, through a washer, and then through a spacer (Illus. 58). Screw this into the hole on the side of the goose. Before repeating this procedure with the other wing section note that if both wings are attached identically to one another they will whirl in the same direction. If one is reversed they will whirl in opposite directions.

After fastening the other wing, cut desired length of the 3/16-in.-diameter metal rod and sand the top of the rod to a dull point with emery cloth. Set the goose on this end and insert the other end into the base or attach the goose outside to fly into the wind.

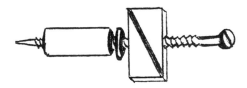

Illus. 58.

Raven

MATERIALS

Pine, ¾ in. thick: 8 × 10 in.
Wooden dowel, ⅝ in. diameter: two
spacers, ⅜ in. long
Metal rod, 3/16 in. diameter: 5 in. long if to
be mounted on a base or 15 to 20 in.
long if not
Flathead wood screws, 1½ in. × 6: two
Washers, SAE ⅛ in.: two
Acrylic paint: mars black, titanium white,
burnt umber, naphthol red light
Brushes: ½ in. and 1/16 in. round
Sandpaper: medium and fine grades
Emery cloth
Semi-gloss lacquer spray
Tracing paper
Poster board

TOOLS

Scroll saw or band saw

Illus. 59.

Drill with 3/32, 5/32, 7/32, and 3/16-in. bits
Stationary belt sander or sanding wheel:
with medium-grade sandpaper
Metal cutters

INSTRUCTIONS

Pattern. Trace the pattern pieces for the
raven and transfer them onto poster
board. Cut out templates, cutting around
the outline only. Trace these patterns
onto the ¾-in. wood.

Cutting. Cut out all raven pieces, making
sure to cut two paddles. Then cut out a 2
× 4½-in. base. Cut two wood spacers, ⅜
in. long, from a ⅝-in. dowel. Before cutting these, drill a 5/32-in.-diameter hole
through the center of the dowel about an
inch deep (Illus. 61).

Drilling. Drill a 5/32-in.-diameter hole
through the center of each paddle. Then,
drill a 3/32-in.-diameter hole through the
raven at the spot indicated on the pattern.
This is where the paddles will be attached.
Drill a hole with the 7/32-in. bit into the
underside of the raven. Final drilling is
done with a 3/16-in. bit through the center
of the base.

Cut off the top ⅜ in. flat head of a tack
or nail with metal cutters and insert this,
flat side out, into the hole on the underside of the raven. Tap it in with a dowel,
using a hammer if necessary.

Shaping Paddles. To form the raven's
paddles, first draw a diagonal line with
pencil from the top right corner to the
bottom left corner on both ends of the
paddle. Each line should be identical. Set

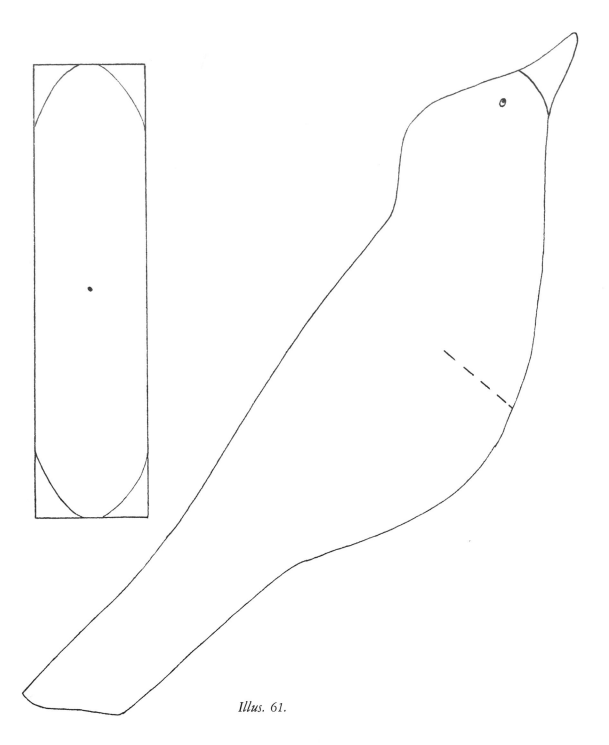

Illus. 61.

both paddles on the table next to each other to check this. Check that both lines are drawn the same and then, without lifting the paddles off the table, carefully turn them around so that the other ends are now facing you. These lines should be at the same left to right angle as the first set.

Take the paddle in your hand and gently press it against the sander. Keep the pencil line *parallel* to the sander at all times. Sand only 1½ in. on each end of the paddle, leaving a center section unsanded. Move the paddle back and forth against the sander, always paying attention to the drawn pencil angle. After you have sanded for a while on one side, sand on the opposite side, working on one end at a time until you have sanded to a thickness of approximately ⅛ to 3/16 in. Repeat this procedure three more times, making the paddles as identical as possible.

Sanding. Sand the edges of the raven's body as round as possible (Illus. 62). Give the paddles and the body a final sanding by hand with fine-grade sandpaper.

Painting. Paint the raven as follows; all measurements are approximate.
Raven, paddles, spacers: 1 tsp. black

Illus. 60.

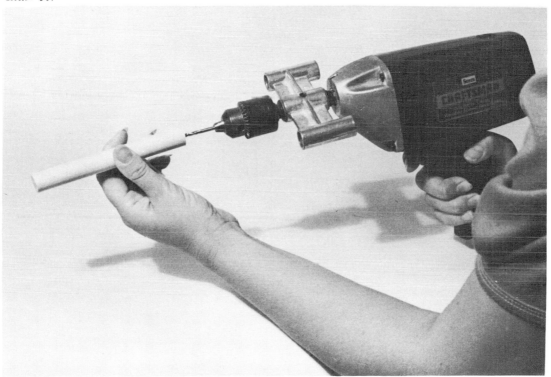

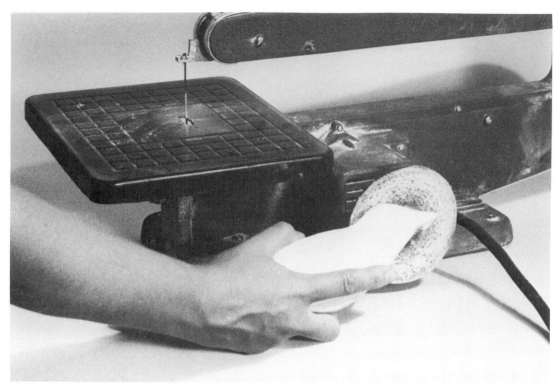

Illus. 62.

Beak, base: ¼ tsp. red/ ¼ tsp. burnt umber

Eye: paint a dot of white/ when dry, paint a smaller dot of black on top of the white dot

Spray with a protective coat of semi-gloss lacquer.

Assembling. Insert a flathead screw through the paddle, through the washer, and then through the spacer (Illus. 58). Screw this into the pre-drilled hole in the raven. Repeat on the other side. If the paddle does not move freely, loosen the screw a little.

Cut a 5-in. length of ³⁄₁₆-in.-diameter metal rod if you are using a base. If not, cut the rod to the desired length according to where your raven will be positioned. Sand the top of the rod to a dull point with emery cloth, then set the raven on this end. Place him on the base or outdoors to fly into the wind.

Wind Toys

Windmill

MATERIALS
Pine, ¾ in. thick: 10 × 12 in.
Pine, ⅜ in. thick: 4 × 4 in.
Wood 2 × 4: 6 in. long
Wooden dowel ³⁄₁₆ in. diameter: 3 in. long
Flathead wood screw, 2 in. × 6: one
Washers, ⅛ in. opening: one ⅜ in., one
½ in.
Metal rod, ³⁄₁₆ in. diameter: 2 in. long
Tracing paper
Poster board
Acrylic paints: titanium white, mars black,
naphthol red light, burnt umber

Illus. 63.

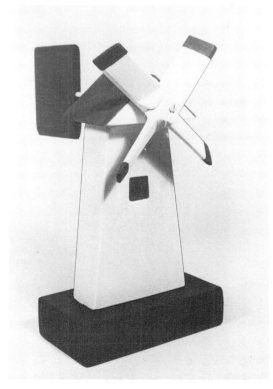

Brushes: ¾ in., ½ in.
Wood glue
Sandpaper: medium and fine grades
Emery cloth
Semi-gloss lacquer spray

TOOLS
Scroll saw or band saw
Drill with ⅛, ³⁄₁₆, ³⁄₃₂, ⁵⁄₃₂, and ⁷⁄₃₂-in. bits
Stationary belt sander or sanding wheel:
with medium-grade sandpaper
Metal cutters

INSTRUCTIONS

Pattern. Trace all the pattern pieces and transfer them onto poster board to make a template. Then trace the windmill building pattern twice onto ¾-in. pine. Trace the pattern for the roof section four times and also two propeller blades onto ¾-in. pine. Transfer the pattern of tail vane onto ⅜-in. wood.

Cutting. Cut one length of 2 × 4, 6 in. long. This is for the base. Cut a length of ³⁄₁₆-in. dowel, 3 in. long. The remainder of the pattern pieces should also be cut.

Gluing. Glue the two building shapes together and the four roof sections together, being as careful as possible to keep them lined up straight. Clamp the pieces together to dry or weight them with a heavy object. Let them dry for at least one hour.

Shaping Paddles. To form the propeller paddles first draw an angle line with pencil from the top right corner to the bottom left corner on both ends of each propeller. Each line should be identical. To check yourself, set both propellers on the table next to each other. Check the first side, which should be the same and then, without lifting the blades off the table, carefully turn them around so that the other ends are now facing you. These lines should be at the same left to right angle as the first. Set one blade on top of the other, keeping the angles as they were, in a cross shape. Mark pencil lines on both blades where they cross one another. Pencil in a ⅜-in. deep area where the blades should be cut out in order to fit together. You may cut this section out either now or after you sand the paddles. It is easiest to cut it out at this stage, but the paddle will not be as strong to work with while sanding. I have done it both ways and have had no problems. You may complete this step using the following instructions for sanding or you may follow the instructions for paddle shaping with the band saw (page 12, General Instructions) and then finish with minor sanding. Be sure to sand or cut away only about 2 in. from each end.

Always pay attention to the drawn pencil angle. Take the paddle in your hand and

Illus. 64.

gently press it against the sander (Illus. 64). Keep the pencil line *parallel* to the sander at all times. Move the blade back and forth against the sander. After you have sanded for a while on one side, sand on the opposite side, working on one paddle at a time until you reach a thickness of approximately ⅛ to 3/16 in. Repeat this procedure three more times, making the paddles as identical as possible since this will affect the operation of your windmill.

Sanding. Sand all other windmill pieces so that they are slightly rounded. Give all pieces a final sanding by hand.

Drilling. Mark the center underneath the roof section. Drill a hole 7/32 in. in diameter. Also mark the center top of the building section and then drill a hole with the 3/16-in. bit. Although the same rod will fit into these two holes, only the top section should have freedom of movement. In the front of the roof section, drill a 3/32-in.-diameter hole in the very center.

Drill a 3/16-in. hole in the center back section and also into the edge of the tail vane where marked. Fit the two propeller blades together and drill a hole with a 5/32-in. bit into the center. Sand the holes smooth.

Painting. Mix the approximate proportions given and paint as follows:
Windmill, propellers: 1½ tsp. white/drop of burnt umber
Roof, tail vane, propeller tips: 1 tsp. red/few drops of black. Also paint a square window in front and a rectangular door in back with this red paint.
Base: ¾ tsp. black

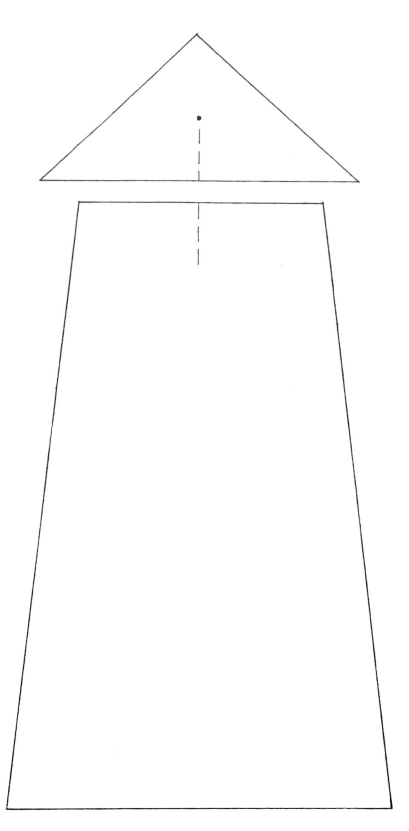

Illus. 65.

Illus. 66.

When dry, spray with a protective coating of semi-gloss lacquer.

Assembling. Glue the windmill to the base and let the glue dry. Cut the top ⅜ in. off of a flathead nail with metal cutters. Insert it into the hole on the underside of the roof section, flat surface facing out.. Tap it into the hole. Cut a 3 in.-length of the 3/16-in. dowel, sand, and insert it into the roof section and tail vane.

Put the 2-in. flathead screw through the propeller, place the ½-in. washer on next and screw it into the front of the roof section. Cut a 2-in. length of 3/16-in. metal rod. Sand the top to a dull point with emery cloth then push rod into the windmill, leaving the point upward. Put the ⅜-in. washer on the rod and then place the roof section on last. If the propeller does not turn freely, unscrew the screw a short distance.

Racing Jockeys

MATERIALS

Pine, ⅜ in. thick: 9 × 16 in.
Pine, ¾ in. thick: 4 × 4 in.
Wood, 1 × 2: 2¼ in. long
Wooden dowel: 3/16 in. diameter, 8 in. long
Acrylic paint: titanium white, burnt umber, naphthol red light, mars black
Stain: medium color
Sandpaper: medium and fine grades
Brushes: ½ in. and ¼ in.
Wood glue
Emery cloth
Semi-gloss lacquer spray

Illus. 67.

Metal rod, 3/16 in. diameter: 15 to 36 in. long, depending on placement
One flathead nail
Tracing paper
Poster board
Base (optional)
    Pine, ¾ in. thick: one piece 6¼ × 7¼ (base)
    Wood finial, any shape: 3 in. diameter, 6 in. high
    Metal rod 3/16 in. diameter: 3 in. long

TOOLS

Scroll saw or band saw
Drill with 3/16-in. and 7/32-in. bit
Stationary belt sander or sanding wheel: with medium-grade sandpaper
Metal cutters

INSTRUCTIONS

Pattern. Trace the pattern pieces, including all paint lines, and transfer them onto poster board to make a template. Cut out outline only and then trace the two jockeys and the large circle onto the ⅜-in. pine. Cut small circle from ¾-in. pine. Mark notches on the large circle.

Cutting. Cut a 1 × 2 block of wood 2¼ in. long. Cut eight ⅛ in. thick strips for the paddles with the band saw. Paddles should be 1 in. wide and 2 in. long. Also cut out the jockeys and circles. Carefully remove the notches of the large circle, cutting two straight cuts and then two diagonal cuts (Illus. 70). Next cut two 4-in. lengths of 3/16-in. dowels. Cut base piece, if desired.

Drilling. Drill holes where marked on the large circle and on the underside of

113

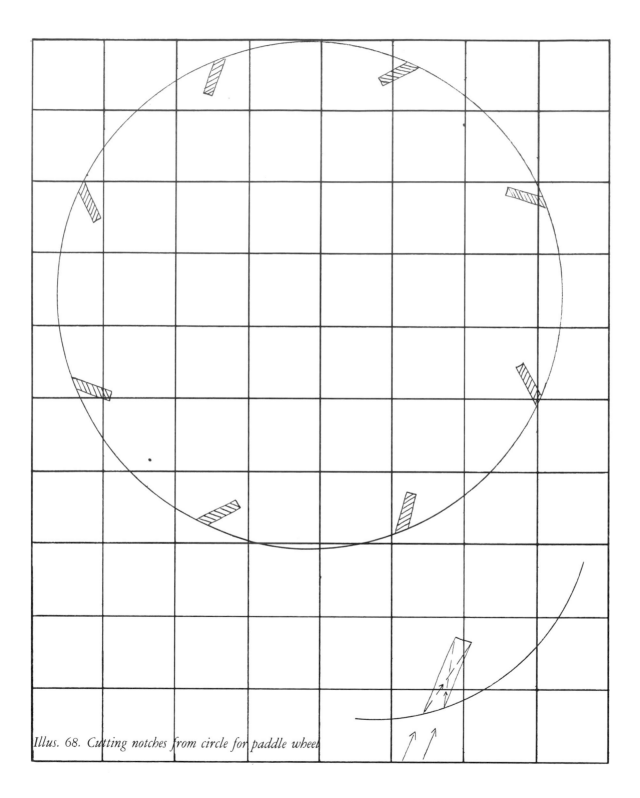

Illus. 68. Cutting notches from circle for paddle wheel

Illus. 69.

the jockeys with a ³⁄₁₆-in. bit. Drill a ⁷⁄₃₂-in.-diameter hole through the center of the small circle. This must be perfectly straight. If you have access to a drill press or drill stand, use it. Drill a ³⁄₁₆-in.-diameter hole in top of the finial. This hole must be centered and straight for perfect balance.

Sanding. Round all edges except paddles with a sander with medium-grade sand-paper. Give all pieces, including the pad-dles, a final sanding with fine sandpaper. Keep the edges of the paddles square.

Paddle Wheel. Insert the paddles into the notches, sanding as needed. Once you are sure they fit, glue them in place (mak-ing sure the top of the paddles are flush with the top of the circle).

Painting. Mix approximate proportions

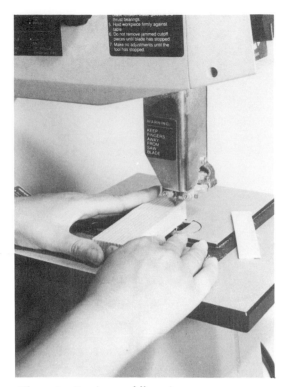

Illus. 70. Cutting paddle strips

No. 2 horse: ¼ tsp. burnt umber/¼ tsp. red

Boots: black

Hair: burnt umber

When dry, spray with a protective coating of semi-gloss lacquer spray

Staining. Apply stain to the base pieces with a small rag, wiping off any excess. Let the stain dry.

Assembling. Glue the small circle to the bottom center of the large circle. Let this dry for approximately one hour. Glue the finial to the base. Cut the metal rod to the length you will be using: 3-in. for base, 15 to 36-in. for outdoors. Sand the end that the paddle wheel will rest on to a dull point using emery cloth. Next, cut off the top ⅜ in. of the flathead nail with metal cutters. Gently turn the paddle wheel over and set the nail head inside the hole of the small circle so the head is on the outside.

Take a scrap of dowel and tap the nail head in. Once it is all the way in tap it with a hammer. Insert dowels into horses and then into the large circle, facing the horses to ride counterclockwise. Place the rod into the bottom of the paddle wheel. This may now be placed on the base, attached to a fence post, mailbox, etc. Your wind toy is finished.

given and paint the parts as follows: Always start with the lightest color and finish with the darkest.

Circles, tails, manes, pants: 1 tsp. white/few drops burnt umber

Paddle tips, caps, jackets: ½ tsp. red/few drops black

No. 1 horse: ¼ tsp. white/¼ tsp. burnt umber

Boy on Bike

MATERIALS

Pine, ¾ in. thick: 11 × 12 in.
Birch plywood, ¼ in. thick: 6 × 8 in.
Sheet metal, copper: .025 × 10 in.
Copper wire, 14 gauge: 15 in. long
Copper or brass rod, ⅟₁₆ in. diameter: 12
in. length
Wooden dowel, ⅝ in. diameter: four ¼
in. lengths
Wooden dowel, ³⁄₁₆ in. diameter: 3 in.
long
Wooden dowel, ⅛ in. diameter: 2 in.
long
Washers, ½ in.: two (with ⅛ in. open-
ing)
Solder
Acrylic paint: titanium white, burnt
umber, chromium oxide green, mars
black, naphthol red light
Brushes: ½ in., ¼ in.

Illus. 71.

Semi-gloss lacquer spray
Sandpaper: medium and fine grades
Emery cloth
Wood glue
Tracing paper
Poster board
Permanent, black, fine-tip marker
For outdoor use: metal rod, ³⁄₁₆ in. diame-
ter: 15 to 36 in. long; Birch plywood, ¼
in. thick: 6 × 8 in.

TOOLS

Scroll saw or band saw: wood cutting
blade and metal cutting blade
Drill with ⁵⁄₆₄, ³⁄₃₂, ⁷⁄₃₂, and ⅛-in. bits
Stationary belt sander or sanding wheel:
with medium-grade sandpaper
Metal cutters
Soldering iron
Needle-nose pliers

INSTRUCTIONS

Pattern. Trace all the pattern pieces, including paint lines, and transfer onto
poster board. Cut out templates, cutting
around the outlines only. Trace body and
wheel section onto ¾-in. pine. Trace two
arms, two thighs, and two foot sections
onto the ¼-in. birch. Trace the wheel pattern onto the copper sheet metal.

Cutting. Cut out all the wood pattern
pieces. Then cut two strips of ¼ in. birch
plywood ½ in. × 7⅜ in. (this is illus-
trated as a pattern piece). Also cut two
base pieces from ¾-in. pine, 1 × 8 in. and
4½ × 10½ in. Cut four ¼-in. lengths of
⅝-in.-diameter dowel, a 3-in. length of ³⁄₁₆-
in. dowel and a 2-in. length of ⅛-in.-di-
ameter dowel. Using the metal cutting
blade, cut out the copper circle, including

Illus. 72.

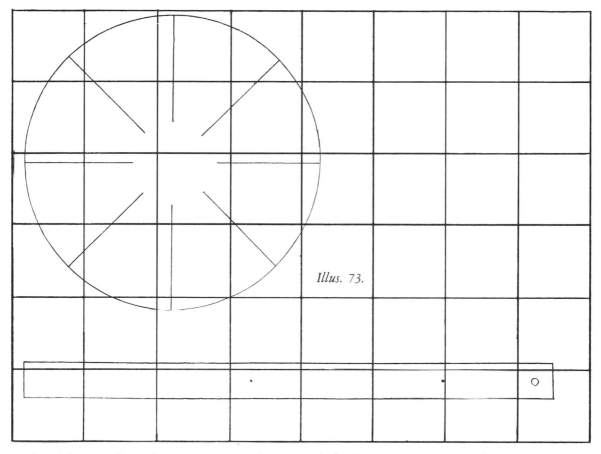

Illus. 73.

the eight cuts into the center section. Sand the edges of the wheel with an emery cloth. Be careful not to scratch the wheel.

Drilling. Drill a ³⁄₃₂-in.-diameter hole in each joint as marked on the patterns and through the top of the 7⅜-in. lengths of birch plywood and the main section of the bicycle where they will be joined. Drill a ⅛-in.-diameter hole into this main section as marked on the curved section. Then drill a ³⁄₃₂-in.-diameter hole through the center of two of the ¼-in. wood spacers previously cut from the ⅝-in. dowel. Then, using the ⁵⁄₆₄-in. bit, drill a

hole through the center of the other two spacers, the center of the copper wheel, the toes of the feet and the point where the axle passes through the 7⅜-in. lengths of birch plywood. Drill a ⁷⁄₃₂-in. hole into the top of this same vertical piece to hold the handlebars.

Sanding. Sand all pieces on the sander, holding the edges at an angle to the sander to achieve a carved effect. Give each piece a final sanding by hand with fine-grade sandpaper. Round edges of the ⅛-in.-diameter dowel and insert into the hole in the curved section of the main bicycle part.

Painting. Paint the wind toy according to the following proportions. Measurements are approximate. Paint lightest areas first, ending with black.
Shirt, socks, 8-in. base piece: ½ tsp. white/ few drops of burnt umber
Hat, pants, 2 spacers (³⁄₃₂-in. hole), trim: ½ tsp. green
Hair, shoes: ⅛ tsp. burnt umber/ drop of red
Bicycle, base: 1½ tsp. black

Spray all pieces with a protective coat of semi-gloss lacquer. When dry, draw the eyes with the black, permanent marker.

Assembling. To form the flared wheel hold the center of the wheel between the thumb and finger of one hand and then, one section at a time, use your thumb and finger of the other hand to gently bend and twist the left side of the section back approximately ³⁄₁₆ in. while you bend and twist the right side of the section forward ³⁄₁₆ in. Do this with each section, making them as identical to the first as you can. Keep the center of the wheel as flat as possible.

Now, cut the ¹⁄₁₆-in.-diameter rod to a 5-in. length and insert this into the center hole of the wheel. Use the soldering iron and solder to fasten the rod to the wheel at the center point of the rod. Slip one of your wood spacers onto the bottom half of the rod and hold the bottom half of the wire with needle-nose pliers to keep the wheel straight while soldering. Hold the wheel in a horizontal position. Make sure the joint is a nice smooth one. Re-

peat this process on the other side of the wheel.

Glue the two base pieces together, making sure the ¾-in. surface is next to the base. It should be 1 in. high.

If you will be using this wind toy outdoors, drill a ⁷⁄₃₂-in.-diameter hole into the underside of the base, drilling about ½ in. into the top base piece. Then cut off the top ⅜ in. of a flathead nail or tack with metal cutters and insert this, flat side out, into this hole. Tap it in with a dowel, using a hammer if necessary.

Then slip a washer on both sides of the wheel and then wood spacers with a ⁵⁄₆₄-in.-diameter hole. Insert the axle into the holes on the vertical pieces of the bicycle. Glue the vertical pieces to the top base piece 1½ in. from the front of this piece and flush with the black base.

Now position the other bicycle piece so that the holes for the cross bar are lined up. Cut and insert a 2¼-in. piece of 14-gauge copper wire. Curl the ends with needle-nose pliers.

Attach the arms of the boy with a 2½-in. length of the copper wire. Curl the ends. Cut a 3½-in. length for the body/leg joint, inserting the green spacers between the body and leg and curl the ends. Cut two 1¾-in. lengths of the copper wire and then drill a ³⁄₃₂-in. hole into the tip of each thigh piece. Insert the 1¾-in. copper wire into the thigh joint and then bend the wire according to the illustration (Illus. 74). The wire bent into the edge of the piece will keep a flat joint next to the bicycle. Flatten the wire against this piece as much as possible. Then insert the other end into the remaining knee piece and curl the end. All joints should be loose enough for free movement.

Round ends of the 3-in. length dowel with sandpaper. Insert this through the holes at the top of the bicycle, sanding sides if necessary. Now position the boy on the bicycle and glue the hands on the handlebars. He should sit back about 1 in. from the vertical pieces. Note that the ⅛-in. dowel protruding from the main section is to keep the knee joints from buckling backwards.

Do not glue the body onto the bicycle until the legs are working properly. Refer to Illus. 75. Bend the rod down at a 90° angle ⅛ in. from the vertical piece. Make another 90° angle away from the bicycle ½ in. from this bend. Slip the feet onto the pedals and check proper movement before making the final bend. Make sure

the wheel does not touch the sides of the bicycle. Make one more 90° angle, ½ in. from the last bend, upward. The first bend on the opposite side of the axle should be upward.

If you are using your boy on the bicycle as a decorative folk toy you can delete the last bend on one of the pedals and use the extended copper rod as a handle to manually make him ride the bicycle.

If he will be riding outdoors, cut a length of a ³⁄₁₆-in.-diameter metal rod. The length depends on where you will place the wind toy. Insert this into the hole underneath the base. The bicycle boy can be left to spin in the wind and catch it as he may, or you may add a tail vane approximately 7 in. long to the base on the left side of the boy. If it is attached to this side, the boy will ride forward. If you decide to use a tail vane, just cut a notch with a coping saw across from the vertical piece and cut a vane from ¼-in. birch plywood.

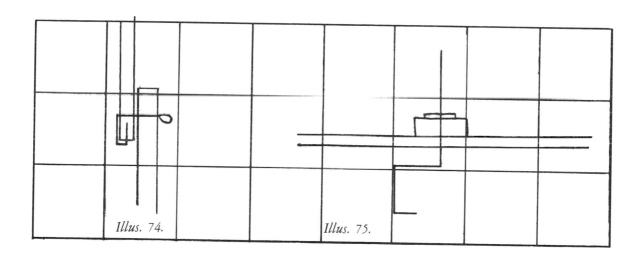

Illus. 74.   Illus. 75.

Man Milking Cow

MATERIALS

Pine, ¾ in. thick: 12 × 12 in.
Birch plywood, ¼ in. thick: 5 × 5 in.
Metal rod, ³⁄₁₆ in. diameter: 15 to 36 in.
long, depending on placement
Wooden dowel, ⅛ in. diameter: 4 in.
long
Wooden dowel, ³⁄₁₆ in. diameter: ¾ in.
long
Brass rod, ¹⁄₁₆ in. diameter: two 12 in.
lengths
Screw eyes, 217 ½: four
Round wood screws ¾ in., ¾ × 4: two
Washers, ⅛ in.: two
Copper tube, ³⁄₃₂ in. opening: one, bought

in 12-in. lengths. This should have an
opening just wide enough for the brass
rod to fit into, yet have room to move.
Solder: miniscule amount
Acrylic paint: titanium white, mars black,
naphthol red light, cerulean blue hue,
turner's yellow, hooker's green, burnt
umber
Brushes: ½ in., ¼ in., and ¹⁄₁₆ in. round
Semi-gloss lacquer spray
Sandpaper: medium and fine grades
Emery cloth
Epoxy glue
Wood glue
Tracing paper
Poster board
Wood scrap, ½ in. square

Illus. 76.

TOOLS

Scroll saw or band saw
Drill with 1/16, 1/8, 5/32, 7/32, and 1/4-in. bits
Stationary belt sander or sanding wheel:
with medium-grade sandpaper
Metal cutters
Soldering iron
Keyhole saw (optional: see cutting instructions)
Needle-nose pliers

INSTRUCTIONS

Pattern. Trace all the pattern pieces and transfer them onto poster board. Set "bending" pattern for the brass rod aside and cut out the remaining templates, cutting around the outline only. Trace the pattern of the base, cow, man, and two propeller blades onto 3/4-in. wood. Trace the tail vane, two arms, and two cow ears onto 1/4-in. birch plywood.

Cutting. Cut out all the pattern pieces. Then drill a 1/4-in. hole into the middle of the circle that is to be cut out of the base. This hole must be cut out with a scroll saw or a keyhole saw. If using the scroll saw, remove one end of the blade and then slip the circle onto the blade. Re-attach the blade and then cut out the circle. Unhook the blade again to remove the base. If you are using a keyhole saw, insert the saw into the drilled hole and cut out the circle. Also cut out the notch in the end of the base. Then, cut three 1/2-in.-lengths of 1/8-in.-diameter dowel. Very carefully, cut two 1/8-in. lengths of copper tubing.

Shaping Propeller. To form the propel-ler paddles, first draw a diagonal line with pencil from the top right corner to the bottom left corner on both ends of each propeller. Each line should be identical. To check yourself, set both propellers on the table next to each other. Check the first side. The lines should be the same. Then, without lifting the blades off the table, carefully turn them around so that the other ends are now facing you. These lines should be at the same left to right angle as the first. Set one blade on top of the other, keeping the angles as they were, in a cross shape. Mark pencil lines on both blades where they cross one another. Pencil in a 3/8-in.-deep area where the blades should be cut out in order to fit together. You may cut this section out either now or after you sand the propellers. It is easiest to cut it out now, but the propeller will not be as strong to work with while sanding. I have done it both ways and have had no problems. You may complete this step using the following instructions for sanding, or you may follow the instructions for paddle shaping with the band saw (see p. 12, General Instructions) and then finish with minor sanding. Be sure to sand or cut away only about 2 in. from each end.

Always paying attention to the drawn pencil angle, take the paddle in your hand and gently press it against the sander. Keep the pencil line *parallel* to the sander at all times. Move the blade back and forth against the sander. After you have sanded for a while on one side, sand on the opposite side, working on one paddle at a time until you reach a thickness of

Illus. 77.

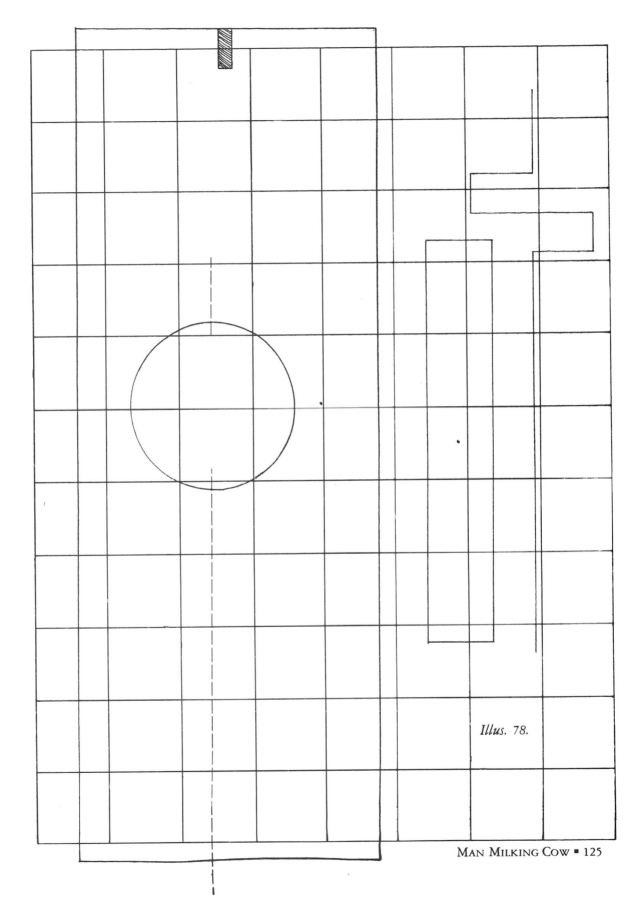

Illus. 78.

approximately ⅛ to 3/16 in. Repeat this procedure three more times, making the paddles as identical as possible since this will affect the operation of your wind toy.

Drilling. Drill a 1/16-in.-diameter hole into the center of the assembled propeller, drilling through both sections at once. This hole should be a snug fit for the brass rod. Then drill a ⅛-in.-diameter hole into the hands of the man and three holes underneath the cow for udders. Use a 5/32-in. bit to drill the shoulders in both the arms and the body. Drill a 7/32-in.-diameter hole through the base, as indicated on the pattern. Also drill a hole with this bit up through the bottom of the man's stool. Cut the top ⅜ in. of a flathead tack or nail with metal cutters and insert this, flat side up, into the hole in the man's stool. Tap it in with a dowel, using a hammer if necessary.

Sanding. Sand edges of all the pieces with the sander. To achieve a carved look, hold the edges at an angle against the sander. Give a final sanding to all pieces by hand, using fine-grade sandpaper. Glue udders into pre-drilled holes.

Painting. Paint pieces according to these approximate proportions.
Cow, tip of propellers and tail vane: ½ tsp. white/ drop of burnt umber
Cow: ¼ tsp. black
Propellers and tail vane, shirt: 1 tsp. red/ drop of black
Pants: ¼ tsp. blue/ drop of black
Boots: drop of black/ drop of white
Hat: ⅛ tsp. yellow

Hair, stool: ⅛ tsp. red/ drop of burnt umber
Base: 1 tsp. green
Cow's udders: ⅛ tsp. white/ drop of red

When all pieces are dry, spray with a protective coat of semi-gloss lacquer.

Assembling. Bend one of the 12-in. lengths of 1/16-in. brass rods according to the pattern. As you bend the rod, slip the two ⅛-in. copper tubing pieces onto each of the "u" sections. (Illus. 79). Now cut two pieces of the other brass rod to approximately 4 in. long. Using needle-nose pliers, curve the end of one of the 4-in. rods around the middle of the copper tubing section. Connect the other rod to the other copper section and then solder each of these curved rods to the copper piece. This will enable the rod to move freely.

Screw the screw eyes into the bottom of the base piece, three evenly spaced on the propeller side of the circle and one just on the other side of the circle. This one should be screwed in after the rod has been inserted. Be sure to put the hanging rods up through the top of the circle. Glue a ½-in. block of scrap wood at the end of the brass rod, closest to the tail vane to keep the mechanism in position.

Fasten the arms to the man with screws, with a washer inserted between the body and the screw. Leave screws loose enough to provide free movement of the arms.

Glue the cow into place, also glue on her ears. Before gluing the man in place, check the position of the rods and insert them into the hands. Bend them just a little while checking the movement of the rods. Spin the rod to make sure the arms are able to move up and down. Make any minor adjustments, then bend the rods over to the sides of the hands and glue the man into place so that both drilled holes coincide.

Glue the tail vane into place with wood glue and then apply a small amount of epoxy glue to the rod where it will hold the propeller. Push the propeller onto the rod. Round the end of the ¾-in. dowel

piece (³⁄₁₆ in. in diameter), drill a ¹⁄₁₆-in.-diameter hole into it and glue it onto the very front of the rod, attaching it to the front of the propeller.

Now cut the ³⁄₁₆-in.-diameter metal rod to your desired length and sand one end of it to a dull point with emery cloth. Insert this end of the pivot rod into the hole through the base and stool. The little farmer should be ready to milk his cow in the wind now. This wind toy can be mounted on a base for indoor appreciation or set up outside for everyone to enjoy.

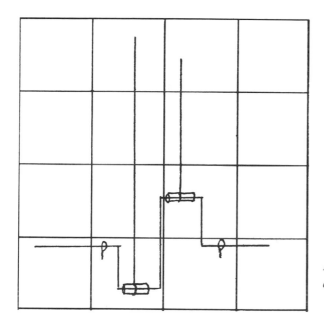

Illus. 79. Bends of brass rods and placement of copper tubing sections

INDEX